FORGIVENESS THERAPY

Breaking the Hidden Power of Bitterness

Overcoming Physical & Psychological Sickness

Venkat Potana

FORGIVENESS THERAPY

Overcoming Physical & Psychological Sickness

Potana
Publications
An Imprint of COACH Trust

Breaking the Hidden Power of Bitterness

Dr. Venkat Potana

Copyright

Title: Forgiveness Therapy: *Overcoming Physical & Psychological Sickness*

Author: Dr. Venkat Potana

ISBN: 978-81-686429-3-5

Date of Publication: 27/04/2026

Christian Outreach and Compassionate Help

Potana Publications: *An Imprint of COACH Trust*

For permissions or correspondence, please contact:
potanabooks@gmail.com

About the Book

This book explores forgiveness not as a single emotional moment, but as a structured inner journey that unfolds through awareness, struggle, decision, repetition, and gradual transformation. It traces how unresolved emotional experiences shape thought patterns, influence the body, and affect everyday living, bringing together practical insight and reflective depth. The thesis of the book is this: "*Unresolved emotional pain and bitterness silently shape the mind, body, and daily life, often leading to inner conflict, emotional sickness, and physical sickness. Forgiveness, practiced as a continuous inner discipline, transforms these patterns by releasing emotional burdens and restoring a person to freedom, stability, and wholeness.*"

Through this lens, the book guides the reader from internal conflict to inner stability, showing how real change develops over time within the mind and emotions. It addresses common misunderstandings about forgiveness and replaces them with a grounded understanding of emotional release, personal responsibility, and sustained inner practice. This work is designed to help readers recognize their own internal patterns and move toward a more peaceful, clear, and stable way of living.

Foreword

In this book Dr. Venkat Potana brings together a rare blend of clinical awareness and human insight in this deeply reflective work on forgiveness and inner healing. Drawing from a background in medical and behavioral sciences, he approaches emotional pain not as an abstract idea, but as something that quietly influences the body, the mind, and the quality of daily living. What makes his writing distinctive is the way he translates complex inner experiences into clear, structured understanding without losing emotional depth.

Throughout this book, Dr. Potana presents forgiveness as a gradual, lived process rather than a single moment of emotional release. His framework moves carefully through awareness, conflict, decision, repetition, and integration, offering readers a realistic pathway that respects both psychological truth and personal experience. This approach reflects a clinician's precision combined with a thoughtful sensitivity to human struggle.

This is a work that speaks to anyone seeking clarity in the midst of emotional weight. It does not rush the reader toward conclusions but instead creates space for understanding to form naturally. Dr. Potana has offered a guide that is both practical and reflective, making this book a meaningful contribution for readers, practitioners, and anyone interested in the connection between emotional healing and everyday life.

—**Dr. Paramjit Singh**
Herbertpur Christian Hospital
April 2026

Dedication

This book is dedicated with respect to **Mr. Bart Howell**, Lead Pastor and Elder of Eagle View Church (EVC) of Fort Worth. Even though I have had only limited interactions, his presence and pastoral leadership reflect a steady commitment to faith, service, and the care of people within the church community.

This dedication is offered in appreciation of that commitment and the encouragement found in those brief moments of connection.

— Dr. Venkat Potana

Contents

Preface

This book emerged from years of engagement as a preacher of the Word, a trainer, a writer, and a counsellor, where I have had the opportunity to observe people across different stages of life and emotional experience. In those settings, one consistent reality became evident: many individuals carry internal burdens that are not always visible on the surface. While life continues outwardly with responsibility and activity, inwardly there are often unresolved emotions, recurring thoughts, and quiet struggles that shape how people think, respond, and relate to others.

As I walked with individuals through conversations, teaching moments, and counselling sessions, a clear need began to surface. Many understood the importance of forgiveness, yet struggled to experience it as a practical inner reality. The challenge was not a lack of desire, but a lack of structured understanding. Forgiveness was often seen as a single act or emotional decision, rather than a process that unfolds over time within the mind, emotions, and daily responses of a person. This gap between understanding and experience became the foundation for this book.

The intention behind this work is to present forgiveness as a journey that can be understood, practiced, and integrated into everyday life. It explores how internal patterns are formed, how they persist, and how they can gradually be reshaped through awareness, decision, and repetition. It also highlights the connection between emotional life, thought processes, and overall well-being, offering a pathway that is both practical and reflective. The aim is not to rush healing, but to bring clarity to the process through which real inner change takes place.

It is my sincere hope that this book will serve as a helpful companion to those seeking greater peace, clarity, and emotional freedom. If it enables readers to better understand their own inner world and take meaningful steps toward lasting transformation, then its purpose will have been fulfilled.

Introduction

The Quiet Weight People Don't Talk About

There are days when everything seems to move in order. Conversations happen, responsibilities are handled, and life appears steady from the outside. Yet within, there is a quiet sense that something is being carried. It is not loud, it is not dramatic, and it does not interrupt the flow of daily life in an obvious way. It sits beneath the surface, shaping the way moments are felt. A person can smile, respond, and continue forward, yet still sense a gentle heaviness that has no clear starting point. It grows out of small experiences that were never fully released. A word spoken carelessly, a moment that felt unfair, a memory that returns without invitation. These do not seem large at the time, yet they leave behind something that remains.

Over time, this quiet weight becomes familiar. It blends into routine and begins to influence how a person sees and responds to the world. Thoughts return to certain places again and again, as if the mind is trying to settle something that never reached rest. Reactions become slightly stronger than expected. Energy feels more limited, even when there is no clear reason for it. Life continues, yet something within feels occupied. Scripture speaks directly to this inner condition with a simple truth: "The spirit of a man will sustain him in sickness, but a wounded spirit who can bear?" (Proverbs 18:14). What is carried inside does not remain hidden. It shapes how life is experienced.

This inner condition rarely draws attention to itself in a direct way. Instead, it expresses itself quietly. A peaceful moment arrives but does not settle deeply. A joyful moment appears but fades more quickly than before. The mind moves forward, yet something keeps pulling backward. A person may not even recognize when this began, yet the effect becomes part of daily life. The Bible brings clarity to this connection when it says, "Keep thy heart with all diligence; for out of it are the issues of life" (Proverbs 4:23). What is held within becomes the source from which everything else flows.

This is where the journey begins. Not in distant ideas, and not in extreme situations, but in the ordinary experience of carrying something unresolved. It is quiet, it is personal, and it is deeply real. Many continue forward without stopping to look at it closely. Yet the moment it is seen clearly, something shifts. Awareness opens the door for change. What has been carried for a long time begins to lose its hidden place. And in that moment, the possibility of a different way of living begins to appear.

The Lingering Presence of Unresolved Moments

There are experiences in life that pass through quickly, and there are others that remain long after the moment has ended. A simple interaction, a brief exchange of words, or a situation that seemed small at the time can continue to live quietly within the mind. Days move forward, new events take place, and yet that earlier moment returns without effort. It does not ask for attention, yet it appears again in thought, as if something within has not yet settled. The person may wonder why such a small thing continues to hold space, yet the presence of it feels real and persistent.

This return of memory does not always follow a clear pattern. It can surface in silence, during routine activity, or even in moments meant for rest. The mind revisits the same scene, sometimes with added emotion, sometimes with new interpretations, and sometimes with a subtle sense of discomfort that has no clear explanation. The experience itself may have been brief, yet what remains feels extended. Scripture speaks to the power of this inner repetition in a reflective way: “As he thinketh in his heart, so is he” (Proverbs 23:7). What the mind continues to hold begins to shape the inner world, even when the original moment has already passed.

Over time, this lingering presence becomes more than a memory. It begins to form a pattern. The same thought returns, the same feeling follows, and the same internal response repeats. What was once a single experience slowly becomes a familiar cycle. A person may begin to anticipate the return of certain thoughts without even realizing it. The mind grows accustomed to revisiting the same emotional space, and this repetition strengthens the sense that the experience is still active, even though it belongs to the past.

In this way, something that started as a moment becomes something that continues as a pattern. It is no longer only about what happened, but about how often it is revisited and how deeply it is held. Scripture gently reveals this unfolding process: “The heart knoweth his own bitterness” (Proverbs 14:10). What remains within begins to take on a life of its own. As this chapter of the journey unfolds, the reader begins to see that what stays longer than it should is not simply a memory, but the beginning of a pattern that quietly shapes the inner life.

How the Inner Tone Begins to Change

Bitterness rarely arrives as a sudden force. It does not begin with intensity or visible expression. It forms quietly, almost gently, through repeated moments that never fully settle. A thought returns, then returns again. A feeling lingers slightly longer than expected. Nothing seems overwhelming at first, yet something begins to shift beneath the surface. The change is gradual. It moves without urgency, without noise, and without drawing attention to itself. A person continues living, speaking, and engaging with others, yet the inner tone begins to carry a different weight than before.

This shift develops through repetition. The mind revisits certain moments, and each return adds a small layer to the emotional response. Over time, these layers begin to shape how situations are interpreted. A neutral moment may feel slightly tense. A simple interaction may carry more meaning than it once did. The emotional response is no longer based only on the present, but also on what has been quietly stored within. Scripture speaks with clarity about this inner process: "Looking diligently lest any man fail of the grace of God; lest any root of bitterness springing up trouble you" (Hebrews 12:15). A root does not appear fully formed. It grows slowly beneath the surface before it becomes visible.

Bitterness, in this early stage, does not always feel like anger. It feels more like a shift in atmosphere. The mind becomes slightly guarded. The heart becomes slightly less open. Trust becomes more cautious. None of these changes seem significant on their own, yet together they begin to shape a new internal climate. A person may not even recognize when this change began, yet its presence becomes part of how life is experienced. Scripture describes this inner influence with simple imagery: "A little leaven leaveneth the whole lump" (Galatians 5:9). A small influence, when repeated, begins to affect the whole.

What makes this stage important is its quietness. There is no clear moment that signals its arrival. It develops without announcement, without interruption, and often without awareness. The person continues forward, unaware that something within has begun to take root. Yet over time, this subtle formation begins to influence thoughts, reactions, and perceptions in ways that feel natural, even though they were not always there. As this journey continues, it becomes clear that what begins quietly can shape deeply, especially when it goes unnoticed.

When Inner Experience Starts Showing in Physical Form

There is a point in human experience where what is carried within begins to express itself through the body. It does not arrive suddenly or dramatically. It appears in small signals that seem unrelated at first. A person notices a tighter chest during ordinary moments, a heavier sense of fatigue after simple tasks, or a restlessness that makes rest feel incomplete. Life continues as normal on the outside, yet the body begins to carry a different kind of strain within its systems.

This connection between inner life and physical experience often develops gradually. Emotional tension does not remain only in thought. It influences sleep, focus, breathing patterns, and energy levels. A person may not immediately link these changes to anything emotional, because the events that caused them may feel distant in time. Yet the body remembers what the mind continues to revisit. Scripture acknowledges this deep unity within human life in a simple way: "A merry heart doeth good like a medicine" (Proverbs 17:22). What is carried internally has measurable influence on physical well-being.

Over time, the repeated return of unresolved thoughts begins to shape physical patterns. Muscles hold tension without clear reason. Rest does not feel fully restorative. Energy rises and falls in ways that seem inconsistent with daily activity. These are not signs of sudden illness, but of a system quietly responding to ongoing internal pressure. The body participates in what the mind continues to process. Scripture also reflects this connection when it says, "My bones waxed old through my roaring all the day long" (Psalm 32:3). Inner struggle does not remain isolated from physical experience.

What becomes clear at this stage is that emotional experience is not separate from physical life. The two operate together in ways that are often unnoticed until patterns become familiar. The body responds not only to external conditions, but also to internal states that persist over time. As this understanding deepens, it becomes evident that what is carried emotionally has a real and steady influence on how the body functions in everyday life.

When the Inner World Becomes Smaller Than It Should Be

There is a form of confinement that does not involve walls, distance, or visible barriers. It develops within the mind through repetition of the same thoughts, the same emotional responses, and the same internal conversations that return without invitation. Life continues outwardly with activity, responsibility, and engagement, yet inwardly something begins to feel narrower. The range of emotional freedom slowly reduces, not all at once, but through patterns that repeat until they become familiar.

In this state, a person may notice that certain situations produce the same reactions again and again. The response feels automatic rather than chosen. A memory appears, and the emotional reaction follows without effort. Over time, this repetition shapes how new experiences are received. Even neutral moments may be filtered through older interpretations. The present becomes influenced by what has already been stored within, and the ability to respond freshly begins to weaken.

Scripture gives a quiet reflection on this kind of inward narrowing when it says, “He that is soon angry dealeth foolishly” (Proverbs 14:17). The emphasis is not only on emotion, but on how quickly internal reactions can take over the space where thoughtful response might have existed. When reactions become automatic, the freedom to pause, reflect, and choose begins to shrink. Another passage adds depth to this idea: “The simple pass on, and are punished” (Proverbs 22:3). There is a movement through life that continues, yet something unseen begins to shape outcomes from within.

This inward narrowing does not stop external life. Work continues, conversations happen, and responsibilities are fulfilled. Yet internally, the sense of openness becomes limited. Thoughts circle familiar paths. Emotional responses follow predictable routes. A person may begin to feel as though certain reactions belong to them permanently, even when they once felt different. What was once flexible becomes fixed through repetition.

At this stage, the idea of an invisible prison becomes clear. It is not formed by external restriction, but by internal repetition that gradually reduces the space of choice. The mind continues to operate, yet within narrower boundaries than before. As this awareness develops, it becomes possible to recognize that freedom is not only about external circumstances, but also about the patterns that shape the inner world.

When Awareness Quietly Breaks the Pattern

There is a moment in many lives when the usual flow of inner experience is gently interrupted. It does not arrive with force or dramatic change. It appears through something simple, like a passing thought that feels different from the usual pattern, a conversation that reflects back something unexpected, or a quiet awareness that arises without being invited. In that moment, the mind pauses in a way it has not paused before. What once felt automatic begins to feel observable.

This interruption is subtle, yet it carries significance. A person begins to notice the difference between what is happening and how it is being experienced. Thoughts that once moved without awareness now become visible to the one thinking them. Emotional responses that once felt immediate begin to show themselves as patterns rather than absolute reactions. Scripture reflects this quiet moment of awareness in a simple truth: “Examine yourselves” (2 Corinthians 13:5). The beginning of change often starts with the ability to observe what has been operating without question.

In this space of interruption, something shifts internally. The mind does not yet change its patterns, but it begins to see them. A sense of distance appears between the observer and the observed experience. A thought arises, and instead of immediately becoming action or emotion, it is seen as something that is happening within. This small gap becomes important, because it introduces the possibility of response rather than reaction. Scripture speaks to this reflective awareness when it says, "Be still, and know" (Psalm 46:10). Stillness creates the space where recognition becomes possible.

This is not a moment of resolution, but a moment of recognition. The patterns that have shaped inner life for a long time begin to come into view. The person does not yet step out of them, but begins to see them from a slightly different position. That shift in perspective marks the beginning of something new. What was once lived unconsciously now becomes visible, and what becomes visible begins to open the way for change. This is the doorway through which the entire journey begins to unfold.

When the Heart Holds Tight to What the Mind Already Sees

There are moments when awareness does not immediately lead to release. Even when a person recognizes what is happening within, something in the emotional world continues to hold tightly. This holding is not random. It is shaped by meaning, memory, and the sense that what was experienced deserves acknowledgment. The mind may begin to understand, yet the inner life continues to protect what feels important, even when it brings discomfort.

This resistance often grows from deeply held ideas of fairness and justice. A person may feel that letting go too soon would reduce the significance of what happened. The emotional system treats the memory as something that must be preserved in order to maintain inner balance. Identity can also become connected to the experience. What happened is not only remembered, but also woven into how a person understands their own story. In this state, releasing the memory feels like releasing part of oneself, even when the intention is to move forward.

Scripture acknowledges this inner tension in a simple way: "The heart knoweth his own bitterness" (Proverbs 14:10). There is a private ownership of emotional experience that cannot be easily dismissed. Another reflection adds depth to this struggle: "For the flesh lusteth against the Spirit" (Galatians 5:17). Within human experience, there are often opposing movements that do not immediately align. One part of the person sees the possibility of release, while another part continues to hold.

Letting go, in this stage, does not feel natural. It can appear as if something important is being overlooked or minimized. The emotional system resists the idea because it interprets release as loss rather than freedom. Even when the mind begins to understand that holding on creates ongoing strain, the inner response does not immediately agree. This is where internal conflict becomes visible, not as confusion to be solved quickly, but as tension that must be acknowledged as part of the process.

Nothing in this moment is resolved yet. Awareness and resistance exist together. Understanding and holding coexist within the same experience. This is not the end of the struggle, but the beginning of seeing it clearly.

The Inner Conflict Intensifies

There is a stage in the inner journey where awareness no longer remains quiet and resistance no longer remains subtle. Both begin to speak at the same time. One part of the inner world begins to long for relief, silence, and a return to ease. Another part continues to hold onto what has been carried, as if releasing it would weaken something essential. These two movements do not cancel each other. They coexist, and in their coexistence, tension becomes more noticeable.

This dual experience creates an internal contradiction that is difficult to ignore. A person may desire peace and still feel connected to the memory of pain. The longing for rest exists alongside the familiar weight of holding on. Inwardly, this feels like standing in two directions at once. The mind leans forward while the heart pulls backward. Neither movement fully disappears, and neither fully wins in this stage. Scripture reflects this divided experience with clarity: “A double minded man is unstable in all his ways” (James 1:8). Instability is not always external. It often begins as an inner division between competing inner responses.

As this tension continues, emotional fatigue begins to appear. Carrying two opposing internal directions requires constant energy. One part of the person is preparing to release, while another part is still reinforcing the need to retain. This ongoing internal negotiation does not remain neutral. It gradually creates weariness. Thoughts feel heavier. Decisions feel slower. Emotional responses begin to feel less clear. The system is not at rest because it is maintaining two different emotional positions at the same time.

Scripture gives language to this inner strain when it says, “A man of a double mind is unstable in all his ways” (James 1:8). Stability becomes difficult when internal direction is divided. Yet this stage is not simply confusion. It is exposure. The tension reveals that something within is shifting, even if it has not yet settled into clarity. What was once hidden conflict now becomes visible experience.

This is where psychological tension reaches its peak before change begins. The mind has not yet resolved the contradiction, but it can no longer ignore it. The weight of holding both movements begins to press inward. In that pressure, the possibility of resolution begins to form, not through force, but through the natural exhaustion of holding two opposing inner realities at once.

Misunderstanding Forgiveness

There are ideas that people resist not because they are truly understood, but because they have been shaped by incomplete or distorted interpretations. Forgiveness is one of those ideas. For many, the word carries assumptions that are not part of its actual meaning, yet these assumptions influence how the heart responds to it. In this way, resistance is often directed not toward forgiveness itself, but toward what it is believed to be.

One common misunderstanding is that forgiveness requires the dismissal of truth. Another is that it demands emotional agreement with what happened. Some associate it with surrendering personal boundaries or weakening moral clarity. Because of these interpretations, the mind can associate forgiveness with loss of control or loss of integrity. The emotional system then reacts defensively, not because forgiveness is understood, but because it is misunderstood. Scripture brings clarity to truth and inner alignment when it says, "Ye shall know the truth, and the truth shall make you free" (John 8:32). Freedom begins where clarity replaces distortion.

Fear plays a significant role in maintaining this misunderstanding. When forgiveness is seen through the lens of loss, the mind naturally resists it. There is concern that releasing emotional holding might weaken accountability or blur the significance of what occurred. This creates a protective response within the inner world. Yet this protection is often directed toward an idea that does not fully represent reality. The result is that the person remains attached not to forgiveness itself, but to a version of it shaped by fear and incomplete understanding.

Because of this confusion, progress becomes difficult. The emotional system continues to respond to an idea that feels threatening, even though the actual concept may be different. The mind holds onto resistance as a form of safety, believing it is preserving truth or identity. Scripture gently challenges this pattern by pointing to the renewing of understanding: "Be ye transformed by the renewing of your mind" (Romans 12:2). Transformation begins when perception is corrected.

At this stage of the journey, clarity becomes the turning point. The resistance is not removed by pressure, but by correction of meaning. Once misunderstanding begins to dissolve, space opens for a different kind of response to emerge. This prepares the mind for what comes next, where forgiveness is no longer something to resist, but something to understand in its true form.

A New Definition Begins to Form

There comes a point where the mind no longer holds only confusion about forgiveness, but begins to see it in a new light. Old interpretations begin to lose their firmness, not through force, but through clarity. What once felt like a single fixed idea starts to separate into distinct parts. The emotional weight that was attached to the word begins to loosen as understanding deepens.

A new recognition begins to form. Forgiveness is not the erasure of memory, nor the denial of what happened. It does not require pretending that pain was never real. Instead, it begins to appear as something internal, something that takes place within the boundaries of the heart and mind. It is experienced as a release of inner holding, where emotional debt no longer governs thought or response. Scripture points toward this inner movement when it says, "Casting all your care upon him; for he careth for you" (1 Peter 5:7). The act of casting reflects an internal transfer, not an external change in history.

As this understanding develops, separation becomes clear between emotional release and moral awareness. A person can remember an event without being bound by it emotionally. Thought and feeling begin to take different paths. The mind learns that acknowledgment of truth does not require ongoing emotional attachment. This distinction creates space where clarity can grow. The idea of forgiveness shifts from something abstract or demanding into something more personal and internal in nature.

This shift does not remove complexity, but it introduces direction. What once felt like a single overwhelming concept begins to open into something understandable and practical. The emotional resistance that was tied to misunderstanding starts to soften as meaning becomes clearer. Scripture reflects this unfolding renewal of perception when it says, "Create in me a clean heart, O God; and renew a right spirit within me" (Psalm 51:10). Renewal begins in how things are seen and understood.

At this stage, forgiveness is no longer only an idea under examination. It begins to feel like a possibility that can be lived. The mind starts to sense that release does not require loss of truth, but instead creates space for a different internal experience. What was once resisted now begins to feel reachable, not as a demand, but as a new way of understanding that is slowly taking shape.

The Turning Point: Decision

There is a stage in the inner journey where explanation is no longer enough. A person has already seen the pattern, recognized the resistance, and understood the meaning more clearly than before. Yet clarity alone does not complete the process. Something more personal begins to emerge, where the focus shifts away from what was done or what was felt, and moves toward what will now be chosen within.

At this point, the question is no longer centered on other people or past events. It becomes internal. The attention turns inward toward the present capacity to decide differently. Emotion continues to exist in its natural form, sometimes aligned with understanding and sometimes not. Yet decision begins to operate on a different level. It does not wait for emotional agreement. It begins to function as a direction chosen by the inner will. Scripture reflects this movement of responsibility with clarity: "Choose you this day whom ye will serve" (Joshua 24:15). Choice introduces direction where emotion may still feel unsettled.

This moment often carries a quiet intensity. The mind recognizes that waiting for perfect emotional readiness may never lead to change. Instead, a different awareness begins to form, where action is no longer dependent on internal comfort. A decision can be made while feelings are still in motion. This distinction becomes important because it separates response from reaction, and intention from emotional fluctuation. In this space, personal agency becomes visible for the first time in a clear way.

As this realization settles, the focus shifts from interpretation to responsibility. What has been understood now calls for a response. The internal conversation becomes less about why things happened and more about what is now within the person's control to choose. Scripture brings this forward with a simple principle: "Let us make a choice" (Deuteronomy 30:19). Life begins to move in the direction of decisions rather than circumstances.

This is the turning point where possibility opens. Nothing external may have changed yet, but internally, the capacity to act differently has appeared. The presence of choice marks the beginning of movement out of repetition and into direction. From this point forward, change is no longer theoretical. It becomes something that can be initiated from within.

When Change First Becomes Felt

There is a stage in the process where change does not announce itself loudly, yet it becomes noticeable in subtle ways. After the moment of decision, life continues in its normal rhythm, but something within begins to feel slightly different. The inner pressure that once felt constant begins to loosen in small degrees. It is not a dramatic transformation, but a gentle easing that can be sensed in everyday experience.

The mind, which once carried repetitive loops of thought, begins to experience moments of silence between those patterns. The same memory may appear, yet it does not hold the same intensity as before. There is a brief space where reaction does not immediately follow thought. In that space, a sense of relief begins to appear, not as a conclusion, but as an early indication that something has started to shift. Scripture reflects this quiet unfolding of inner change when it says, "Be still, and know" (Psalm 46:10). Stillness becomes the place where subtle transformation can first be recognized.

This early change is often difficult to define, yet it is difficult to ignore once noticed. The emotional weight that once felt constant begins to fluctuate. Certain moments feel lighter than expected. Internal responses feel less sharp, less immediate, and less consuming. The system has not fully settled, yet it no longer feels entirely the same. This creates a new kind of awareness where comparison becomes possible between what was and what is beginning to emerge.

At this stage, hope begins to form in a quiet and grounded way. It does not rely on full resolution or complete understanding. Instead, it arises from the simple recognition that change is already in motion. Scripture captures this emergence of hope in a steady way: "The path of the just is as the shining light, that shineth more and more unto the perfect day" (Proverbs 4:18). Progress is not always immediate, but it is directional.

What makes this moment important is its honesty. It does not claim that everything is resolved, yet it also does not remain in the previous state. A shift has occurred that can be felt rather than explained. In that subtle difference, the foundation for deeper transformation begins to take shape, carrying forward a quiet assurance that change is real and continuing.

Why Letting Go Is a Process

There is a stage in inner change where progress does not follow a straight line. A person may experience moments of relief, clarity, and peace, yet the same thoughts can return without warning. The mind revisits familiar scenes, familiar words, and familiar emotions, even after a sincere decision has been made to move forward. This return does not mean nothing has changed. It reflects how deeply patterns can remain active while new direction is still forming.

These returning thoughts often carry emotional echoes. The intensity may be less than before, yet the presence of the memory still feels real. In some moments, it can seem as though progress has paused or reversed. However, what is actually taking place is a process of repetition that slowly reshapes response. The mind is learning a new way of relating to what it once held tightly. Scripture gives language to this ongoing inner renewal when it says, “Though the outward man perish, yet the inward man is renewed day by day” (2 Corinthians 4:16). Renewal is described as something continuous rather than immediate.

In this stage, forgiveness is no longer understood as a single event that completes everything at once. It becomes a repeated practice of release. Each time the thought returns, there is another opportunity to respond differently. Sometimes the response is strong, sometimes it is weak, and sometimes it is simply awareness without reaction. Over time, these repeated moments begin to reshape the inner direction. What once felt automatic begins to loosen through repetition.

This ongoing process does not indicate failure. It reflects how internal change naturally develops over time. Emotional systems do not reorganize instantly. They adjust through repeated experiences of choosing differently. Scripture acknowledges this steady formation when it says, “Be not weary in well doing” (Galatians 6:9). Persistence becomes part of transformation.

At this point in the journey, the expectation of instant completion gives way to a more realistic understanding. Letting go is not a single step but a continuing movement. Each return of thought becomes part of the process rather than a disruption to it. In this way, repetition becomes not an obstacle, but the environment in which lasting change is formed.

The Mind Begins to Heal

There is a stage in inner change where the most noticeable shift appears not in external circumstances, but in the quality of thought itself. The mind begins to feel less crowded. Thoughts still arise, but they no longer overlap in the same way or pull attention in multiple directions at once. The internal environment starts to feel more organized, as if space has opened where there was once constant activity.

One of the first signs of this shift is a reduction in mental repetition. Situations that once triggered continuous replay begin to lose some of their pull. The mind may still remember, but it does not remain fixed in the same cycle for as long. Moments of quiet appear more naturally. Between thoughts, there is a sense of stillness that was not as present before. Scripture reflects this inner settling when it says, “Be still, and know that I am God" (Psalm 46:10). Stillness becomes more than a concept; it becomes an experienced state within thinking itself.

As clarity increases, decisions begin to feel less emotionally entangled. The mind can observe situations with greater distance. This does not mean emotion disappears, but it no longer dominates interpretation. Thought becomes more structured, less reactive, and more grounded in present awareness rather than past repetition. The internal narrative loses some of its urgency, allowing space for clearer perception of what is actually happening in the moment.

Another noticeable change is the reduction of rumination. The mind no longer returns to the same memory with the same intensity or frequency. When it does return, it tends to release more quickly rather than continuing the loop. This shift creates a more stable internal rhythm, where attention is not constantly pulled backward. Scripture speaks to the renewing nature of this transformation: "Be renewed in the spirit of your mind" (Ephesians 4:23). Renewal becomes visible in how thought patterns reorganize themselves over time.

What emerges at this stage is not perfection, but stability. The mind begins to function with less internal conflict and more coherence. Thought becomes easier to follow, easier to release, and less emotionally charged. This measurable change in thinking patterns marks a clear sign that internal healing is no longer theoretical. It is actively reshaping how the mind operates from within.

The Body Follows the Mind

There is a stage in the process where changes in thought and emotion begin to show their influence beyond the mind. The body, which has carried tension for a long time, starts to respond to the new internal atmosphere. This does not happen all at once, and it does not appear in dramatic form. It is observed gradually, through everyday experiences that feel slightly different from before.

One of the first signs is a reduction in physical tension. Muscles that were previously held tight begin to soften in subtle ways. Breathing becomes less shallow, and the sense of internal pressure begins to ease during ordinary moments. Sleep, which may have been irregular or restless, begins to feel more continuous. These changes are not forced; they appear as the body adjusts to the reduction of internal emotional strain. Scripture reflects this connection between inner state and physical life in a simple way: "A merry heart doeth good like a medicine" (Proverbs 17:22). What is carried within influences the condition of the whole person.

As emotional burden decreases, energy begins to return in a more stable form. The fatigue that was once tied to internal conflict begins to lessen. Daily tasks feel less draining, not because circumstances have changed, but because the internal load has shifted. The body is no longer constantly responding to the same level of emotional tension, and this creates space for recovery. Rest begins to feel more restorative, allowing the system to rebuild rather than simply pause.

Another noticeable change is the improvement in overall resilience. The body no longer reacts as sharply to small stressors. There is a greater sense of balance in physical responses, as if the system is no longer operating under constant internal strain. Scripture acknowledges the harmony between inner state and physical strength when it says, "A sound heart is the life of the flesh" (Proverbs 14:30). Inner peace contributes to bodily stability in ways that become increasingly evident over time.

At this point, the connection between emotional freedom and physical experience becomes clearer. The body is not separate from the inner world; it reflects it. As the mind becomes less burdened and emotional cycles begin to settle, the body follows with its own form of restoration. What begins internally gradually becomes visible in the physical life, showing that healing is not limited to thought or feeling alone, but extends to the whole person.

Relationships Begin to Shift

There is a stage in personal transformation where internal change begins to influence the way relationships are experienced. This influence does not appear in uniform form. Some connections begin to soften, communication becomes easier, and misunderstandings lose some of their intensity. In other cases, distance remains, and interaction does not return to what it once was. Both outcomes can exist at the same time without contradiction.

As emotional patterns change within a person, the way they respond to others also begins to shift. Conversations that once carried tension may feel less charged. Situations that previously triggered strong reactions begin to feel more manageable. At the same time, not every relationship follows the same direction. Some remain unchanged in structure, and some naturally separate. This variation is part of how human connections respond to internal change.

Scripture reflects the value of peace in relationships while also recognizing personal responsibility in maintaining inner stability. "If it be possible, as much as lieth in you, live peaceably with all men" (Romans 12:18). This statement acknowledges both effort toward harmony and the limits of what depends on one person alone. It establishes that peace is pursued, not controlled entirely by outcome.

At this stage, an important understanding begins to form: emotional freedom and relational boundaries can exist together. A person can experience internal release from resentment while still maintaining appropriate distance where needed. Forgiveness does not require continued exposure to harmful patterns. Instead, it allows the inner world to remain free while the outer structure of relationships adjusts according to wisdom and discernment.

Another reflection of this balance appears in the idea that growth sometimes changes the nature of connection itself. Some relationships evolve into healthier forms, while others remain at a distance without emotional burden. Both outcomes can be held without inner conflict. What matters most is that the internal state is no longer dictated by external behavior.

At this point in the journey, freedom is no longer dependent on relational outcome. Boundaries become a form of clarity rather than separation driven by emotion. Peace within is no longer fragile or conditional. It exists alongside wisdom in how relationships are held, showing that emotional freedom and healthy limits can coexist without contradiction.

Identity Transformation

There is a stage in inner change where the deepest shift is not in behavior or emotion alone, but in identity itself. This is not a surface adjustment. It is a reorganization of how a person understands themselves at the core. The past still exists as memory, but it no longer functions as the defining center of who the person is becoming. A new sense of self begins to take shape quietly and steadily.

In earlier stages, identity may have been closely connected to what was endured. Experiences of pain, loss, or offense can begin to influence how a person describes themselves internally. Without realizing it, the memory of what happened can become part of how life is interpreted. At this stage, however, that connection begins to loosen. The person starts to notice that what happened is part of their story, but not the totality of their identity. Scripture speaks to this reorientation of identity with clarity: “If any man be in Christ, he is a new creature” (2 Corinthians 5:17). The emphasis is on becoming, not being defined by what came before.

As this transformation deepens, emotional independence begins to develop. Reactions are no longer governed by past wounds in the same automatic way. Situations may still carry emotional significance, but they do not determine self-worth or internal stability. There is a growing ability to remain steady even when external triggers appear. This does not erase memory, but it changes the authority memory once held over present identity.

Another important change is the reduction of internal labeling. The mind no longer repeatedly returns to past definitions of self shaped by hurt or limitation. Instead, there is space for a more stable and present understanding of identity to form. This shift is not forced; it emerges gradually as emotional cycles lose their dominance. Scripture reflects this renewal of inner identity when it says, “Be renewed in the spirit of your mind” (Ephesians 4:23). Renewal is not only about thought patterns, but also about self-perception.

At this point, a major turning point becomes clear. The person is no longer primarily living from the memory of what was endured, but from the awareness of what is now possible. Identity is no longer anchored in past injury, but in present stability. This marks a deep internal transition where emotional independence begins to support a more grounded and consistent sense of self.

Living Differently Every Day

There is a stage in inner transformation where change no longer feels like a series of separate breakthroughs. Instead, it begins to appear in ordinary daily life. The way a person responds to small moments, interruptions, and unexpected words starts to reflect a different internal structure. What once required effort becomes more natural over time, not because circumstances have become easier, but because the internal response has been reshaped.

In daily interactions, there is a noticeable difference in how quickly emotional reactions settle. Situations that once might have lingered in the mind begin to pass through with less resistance. The pause between stimulus and response becomes more available. This creates space for intentional choice rather than automatic reaction. Scripture reflects the value of steady inner life when it says, “Let your moderation be known unto all men” (Philippians 4:5). Stability is expressed through consistent conduct rather than occasional effort.

As this pattern continues, habits of thinking begin to shift. The mind becomes less inclined to revisit offense repeatedly. Even when difficult thoughts appear, they are less likely to develop into extended emotional cycles. Attention moves more easily toward constructive or neutral directions. This does not mean that challenges disappear, but the internal engagement with them becomes more balanced and less consuming.

Over time, release becomes faster and more familiar. What once required prolonged struggle begins to happen with greater ease. This is not the result of suppression, but of repeated internal practice that has shaped new pathways of response. Scripture speaks to the formation of steady character when it says, “He that is faithful in that which is least is faithful also in much” (Luke 16:10). Consistency in small moments builds strength in larger ones.

At this stage, sustainability becomes visible. Change is no longer dependent on intensity or emotional highs. It is maintained through ordinary living. The transformation has moved from isolated experiences into a continuous pattern of life. What is seen now is not occasional improvement, but a stable direction that holds across time and situations, showing that inner change has become integrated into everyday existence.

The Cost of Not Changing

There is a point in reflection where a person begins to see not only what change can bring, but also what remains the same when change is delayed. Life continues outwardly, responsibilities are met, routines are maintained, yet internally the same emotional patterns can quietly repeat. The mind returns to familiar thoughts, familiar interpretations, and familiar reactions. Over time, what was once a response to specific events can become a general way of experiencing life itself.

When emotional cycles are not interrupted, they often become more automatic with time rather than less. The same memories continue to surface, and the same internal reactions tend to follow them. Even when circumstances shift, the inner response can remain unchanged. This creates a sense of repetition that affects clarity and focus. Scripture describes the condition of a divided inner life when it says, “A double minded man is unstable in all his ways” (James 1:8). Instability is often experienced not in a single moment, but in patterns that repeat over time.

As these cycles continue, the sense of inner peace becomes less consistent. Moments of calm may still appear, but they are often interrupted by familiar emotional patterns that reassert themselves. Mental energy is gradually drawn into managing internal repetition, which can limit the sense of clarity and presence in daily life. Over time, this can influence how situations are perceived, making it more difficult to respond with freshness or openness.

Another effect of remaining within unchanged patterns is the gradual reduction of internal space for rest. When the mind repeatedly revisits unresolved emotional material, it requires ongoing attention, even if unconsciously. This can affect overall vitality and attention. Scripture offers a contrasting picture of settled inner life when it says, “In returning and rest shall ye be saved; in quietness and in confidence shall be your strength” (Isaiah 30:15). Rest is presented as a condition of stability rather than struggle.

At this stage of understanding, urgency arises not from pressure, but from recognition. The cost of remaining unchanged is not a sudden event, but a gradual shaping of experience over time. Peace, clarity, and energy are not lost in a single moment; they are slowly diminished when inner patterns remain unaddressed. This awareness brings focus to the importance of direction, not through fear, but through honest observation of what continued repetition produces in the inner life.

The Invitation

There comes a point where reflection stops being about ideas and begins to become personal. What has been described across these pages is no longer only a pattern observed in others or a concept understood intellectually. It begins to meet the reader in the quiet space where private thoughts are formed. This is where the journey naturally turns inward, not as a demand, but as an invitation to notice one's own inner world with honesty.

At this stage, questions arise that cannot be answered on behalf of someone else. They are simple, yet they carry depth. What memories still hold emotional weight when they appear without warning. What thoughts return most often when silence increases. What internal reactions feel automatic rather than chosen. These questions are not meant to create pressure, but to create awareness of what is already present within daily experience. Scripture reflects this moment of self-examination when it says, "Examine yourselves" (2 Corinthians 13:5). The invitation is toward clarity rather than comparison.

As awareness deepens, the reader is gently brought into participation with the material rather than remaining an observer of it. The journey described is not distant from ordinary life. It is formed within it, through the small and repeated moments that shape how each day is experienced. In this sense, the story does not conclude outside the reader, but continues within their own reflection, choices, and awareness.

This moment is not designed to close anything, but to open space for consideration. There is no urgency imposed and no conclusion forced. Instead, there is a quiet recognition that every person holds within them the capacity to respond differently to what has been carried. Scripture expresses this openness of response when it says, "Behold, I have set before thee an open door" (Revelation 3:8). An open door does not compel entry; it simply makes passage possible.

What remains at the end of this introduction is not pressure, but possibility. The material has traced patterns of inner life, but the final movement belongs to the reader alone. The invitation stands quietly in the background of awareness, asking only for honest reflection and personal consideration. From here, the next step is not defined by instruction, but by choice.

Chapter 1: The Sense of Incompleteness

When the Past Lives Inside the Present

In January 1945, in the final days of World War II, the Auschwitz concentration camp in Nazi-occupied Poland was liberated by Soviet forces. Among the survivors were two young Romanian Jewish twins, Eva Mozes and Miriam Mozes, born on January 31, 1934. They had been subjected to the medical experiments of Josef Mengele, known infamously as the "Angel of Death." Their childhood was not defined by normal development, but by systematic trauma inside one of history's most documented centers of human suffering.

After liberation, Eva Mozes Kor carried her survival into adulthood, but survival did not mean internal peace. Like many Holocaust survivors, she lived with long-term psychological consequences of trauma: recurring nightmares, emotional distress, and what modern psychology would later identify as trauma-related stress responses. She built a life, married, moved to the United States, and raised a family, yet beneath the surface there remained something unresolved—not only memory of what happened, but the internal pressure of what had never been released.

For decades, Eva lived with deep anger toward the Nazi regime and toward Josef Mengele in particular. That anger was not abstract; it shaped her internal world. It influenced how memory was processed, how trust functioned, and how the past remained active inside present consciousness. Even when external life appeared stable, internally there was a continuing sense of incompleteness, as if part of her emotional life was still anchored in Auschwitz.

In 1995, during a public Holocaust remembrance event in Israel, Eva Mozes Kor made a decision that would later become widely documented and debated: she publicly forgave the Nazis, including Josef Mengele. She stated that forgiveness, for her, was not about excusing what had happened, nor about denying history, but about releasing the emotional burden she had carried for decades. In her own reflections over the years, she consistently described this act not as forgetting, but as personal liberation from long-held internal pain.

What followed, according to her public testimony and later interviews, was not an instant erasure of memory, but a noticeable shift in her internal emotional state. The intensity of anger that had accompanied the memory began to loosen its grip. She described experiencing a form of relief—less emotional reactivity tied to recollection, and a reduced sense of being internally controlled by the past. The events remained part of her history, but their emotional authority over her present life diminished.

This does not rewrite what she endured. Nothing about forgiveness changed the historical truth of Auschwitz, nor did it undo the reality of what was done. But it did alter something equally significant: the way that memory continued to live inside her. What once functioned as a constant source of internal emotional activation gradually became a memory that no longer dictated her present identity in the same way.

Her experience stands as a documented example often referenced in trauma and forgiveness studies, illustrating a distinction between memory and ongoing emotional captivity. It shows that human beings can continue to carry factual history without being continuously governed by its emotional weight. In psychological terms, this reflects a shift from unresolved emotional processing to integrated memory—where the past remains known, but no longer dominates internal functioning.

The sense of incompleteness that begins this chapter is precisely this internal condition: when life continues outwardly, but something inside remains unfinished, repeatedly activated by memory that has not been released. Eva Mozes Kor's journey does not erase suffering, nor does it simplify justice. Instead, it reveals something more subtle and deeply human—the possibility that the inner world can remain bound long after external events have ended, and that release, when it occurs, changes not history, but the way history continues to live within a person.

That is where this chapter begins: not with theory, but with a lived human reality where survival is not the same as inner completion, and where forgiveness becomes not a moral abstraction, but an internal turning point in how a person continues to carry their own life.

****

In the city of Minneapolis in the year 1993, a woman named Mary Johnson faced a moment that would shape the rest of her life in ways she never expected. Her son, Amir Johnson, only twenty years old, was shot and killed during a gang confrontation. The pain of that loss settled deep within her heart, and with it came a wave of anger that seemed justified, powerful, and unrelenting. The young man responsible, Oshea Israel, was arrested and sentenced to prison, and from that moment forward Mary carried within her a storm that refused to quiet. The grief did not remain only in her thoughts. It began to shape her days, her reactions, her physical strength, and her sense of peace. Every memory of her son brought both love and pain, and every thought of the man who caused his death stirred something heavy and consuming within her. Over time, she began to realize that the anger she held had become a constant presence, touching every part of her life and refusing to loosen its grip.

As the years passed, Mary noticed something deeper unfolding within her. The anger that once felt like a form of strength had slowly turned into a burden that followed her everywhere. It entered her quiet moments, interrupted her rest, and colored her view of the world around her. She found herself thinking about the past again and again, reliving the loss, carrying the weight as though it had just happened. Researchers today describe this kind of emotional state as one that triggers ongoing stress within the body, releasing tension that affects both mental and physical health over time. Mary did not need a study to tell her what she felt. She knew that something inside her had become heavy, something that no amount of time alone seemed to heal. The bitterness she carried did not change what had happened, yet it continued to shape what she felt, how she lived, and how she moved through each day.

Then a turning point began to form, quietly at first, then with growing clarity. Mary came to a realization that shifted everything within her. She saw that the anger she carried had begun to take more from her than the original loss itself. It had entered her peace, her strength, and her ability to live freely. In that moment, she made a decision that would seem impossible to many. She chose to forgive. Years later, she met Oshea Israel face to face, spoke with him, and eventually formed a relationship built on grace rather than resentment. The transformation that followed did not erase her loss, yet it changed the weight she carried within. Where bitterness once ruled, a new kind of freedom began to take root. “Let all bitterness, and wrath, and anger, and clamour, and evil speaking, be put away from you, with all malice.” (Ephesians 4:31).

The Public Image

There are seasons in life where the outward presentation of a person becomes so consistent that it begins to define how others interpret their entire existence. Strength becomes expected, stability becomes assumed, and a quiet sense of confidence is attributed to every word and action. In such moments, a life can appear fully composed, even while something deeper remains unseen and unspoken. The public image grows slowly, shaped by responsibility, routine, and the natural desire to be perceived as capable in a world that measures value through performance and appearance. Yet what is visible to others often tells only a fraction of the truth that lives within.

The Life Everyone Admired

There was a steady recognition that followed me in many environments, where people responded to me with trust, respect, and a sense of assurance that I would handle whatever was placed before me. My life appeared organized in a way that suggested control and maturity, and many conversations naturally turned toward accomplishments, duties fulfilled, and the reliability I was believed to carry. I learned to navigate these expectations with ease, presenting a version of myself that aligned with what others needed to see in order to feel confident in my presence.

Within this outward rhythm, I became accustomed to maintaining composure regardless of what I experienced internally. The discipline required to sustain such an image was not always visible, yet it shaped my daily interactions in subtle ways. Words were chosen carefully, expressions were managed thoughtfully, and emotional weight was often set aside in order to preserve the stability others had come to associate with me. "Man looketh on the outward appearance, but the Lord looketh on the heart." (1 Samuel 16:7).

Over time, I began to recognize a quiet separation forming between perception and reality. The admiration of others remained consistent, yet it did not fully reflect the inner experience that accompanied each day. While life continued in an orderly and productive manner on the surface, there was another layer of awareness developing within me, one that observed the difference between how life appeared and how it was actually being lived. This growing awareness marked the beginning of a deeper understanding that would slowly unfold beyond the reach of public view.

The Private Weight

There are burdens that do not announce themselves with visible signs, yet they settle quietly within the inner world of a person and begin to shape the way each day is experienced. While outward life continues with structure and expectation, another dimension develops beneath the surface, where thoughts grow heavier and emotions become more difficult to name. In that hidden space, silence begins to carry meaning, and even moments of stillness feel filled with unspoken pressure. What others interpret as calmness is often the result of holding together what feels internally scattered, and over time, this quiet effort becomes a weight that accompanies every interaction.

When Silence Became Heavy

After public interactions, when the appearance of composure was no longer required, there often came a subtle sense of depletion that was difficult to explain. It was not the result of physical exhaustion alone, but something deeper that touched the emotional core. The effort required to maintain stability in front of others would leave behind a lingering stillness that felt dense and unprocessed. In those moments, silence was no longer peaceful; it became something that pressed inward, revealing that more had been carried throughout the day than was acknowledged in real time.

As this pattern continued, emotional fatigue began to surface in ways that could not easily be dismissed. There was a growing awareness that presenting strength required a level of internal effort that remained unseen by those around me. Each time I appeared composed, attentive, and engaged, a part of my inner life had been set aside in order to maintain that outward presence. The return to solitude often revealed the cost of that effort, as though something essential had been quietly spent in exchange for appearing "fine." "Man looketh on the outward appearance, but the Lord looketh on the heart." (1 Samuel 16:7).

Within this unfolding experience, a contradiction began to form between external expression and internal reality. On the surface, life continued in a structured and responsible manner, yet within, there was a growing awareness that something was not fully aligned. The consistency others observed did not match the internal fluctuations that were becoming more noticeable with each passing day. This contradiction did not arrive suddenly; it developed gradually, through repeated cycles of engagement and withdrawal, until it became clear that two different experiences of life were existing simultaneously within the same person.

As this awareness deepened, the private weight became more than a passing sensation. It became a steady presence that accompanied reflection, decision, and even rest. The effort to maintain outward stability began to reveal its internal cost, and the silence that followed each day began to speak with increasing clarity. What had once been dismissed as simple tiredness was now recognized as something more layered, something that pointed toward an inner condition that required attention, understanding, and eventually transformation.

The First Signs in the Body

There comes a point in inner struggle where thoughts and emotions begin to extend their influence beyond the mind and quietly enter the physical experience of life. What is carried internally does not remain confined to reflection alone, but gradually expresses itself through subtle changes in strength, rhythm, and energy. The body, in its own language, begins to register what the heart has not fully expressed. In this way, what is unseen in emotion slowly becomes visible in physical sensation, revealing that the human being is not divided into separate parts, but deeply interconnected in ways that often go unnoticed until tension begins to surface.

When the Body Begins to Speak

The earliest signs appeared in ordinary moments, almost unnoticeable at first, yet consistent enough to draw quiet attention. Rest no longer felt complete, as sleep carried interruptions that left mornings feeling unfinished and heavy. There was a persistent sense of tightness within, as though the body itself was responding to an ongoing internal pressure that had not yet been addressed. Fatigue began to arrive earlier in the day, even after routine activity, and irritability surfaced in moments that previously would have passed without reaction. These experiences were not dramatic on their own, yet together they formed a pattern that suggested something deeper was unfolding beneath the surface of daily life.

As time continued, it became clearer that the body was responding with greater honesty than the mind was willing to acknowledge. While outward reasoning attempted to maintain order and stability, physical sensations began to reveal what had been quietly accumulating within. The body seemed to carry awareness ahead of conscious recognition, expressing through tension what had not yet been fully understood in thought. “A merry heart doeth good like a medicine.” (Proverbs 17:22). In contrast, a burdened heart began to reveal its presence through the language of strain, fatigue, and restlessness that could not easily be explained away.

This growing awareness introduced a deeper realization that emotional suppression does not remain confined to feeling alone. What is repeatedly held back in expression does not disappear; instead, it begins to translate into physical experience, creating pressure where there was once ease. The internal effort to remain composed and unaffected gradually shaped the condition of the body, until the distinction between emotional state and physical response became increasingly difficult to separate. In this unfolding awareness, the body became a quiet witness, reflecting truths that had not yet been fully spoken within.

The Hidden Emotional Pattern

There is a layer of human experience where events from the past do not remain in the past at all, but continue to live in memory with surprising persistence. Even when life moves forward in practical terms, the mind can quietly revisit moments that carried emotional weight, returning to them without invitation. These inner returns often feel natural at first, almost familiar, yet over time they begin to reveal a pattern that shapes perception, mood, and response in subtle ways. What appears settled on the outside can remain active within, creating an ongoing internal movement that is not always visible to others.

Replaying What Should Have Been Forgotten

Certain conversations would return in silence, unfolding again in the mind with different endings imagined, different words considered, and different outcomes rehearsed. What had already taken place externally would continue internally as though the moment still required resolution. At times, entire dialogues would form within, where responses were crafted long after the opportunity for exchange had passed. These silent repetitions did not bring closure; instead, they extended the life of the experience far beyond its original moment, keeping emotional energy engaged with what had already occurred.

Within these mental repetitions, an internal tension began to develop, shaped by unresolved emotional exchanges that had never found completion. The mind would revisit what was said, what was left unsaid, and what might have been said differently, creating a cycle that quietly reinforced itself. These patterns did not require external triggers to begin; they would arise spontaneously in moments of stillness, reflection, or even routine activity. Over time, this created a background current of thought that influenced emotional tone without clear awareness of its presence. “As he thinketh in his heart, so is he.” (Proverbs 23:7).

As this pattern continued, the sense of inner rest began to shift. What once felt like neutral memory became emotionally active experience, carrying weight that extended into present awareness. The mind, without intention, would return again and again to the same unresolved points, as though seeking completion through repetition alone. This ongoing cycle created an internal environment where tension could exist without an identifiable cause in the present moment, revealing that emotional life is often shaped as much by remembered experience as by current reality.

The False Stability

There are periods in life where continuity becomes the most convincing evidence of stability. Responsibilities are fulfilled, routines are maintained, and relationships continue without visible disruption. From the outside, everything appears to move in an orderly rhythm, as though each part of life is functioning exactly as expected. This outward flow creates an impression of consistency that others naturally rely upon, while the internal experience remains something far more complex and less easily observed. In such seasons, life can appear steady even when deeper layers are quietly unsettled.

Life Continued as Normal

Work continued with the same level of responsibility and attention that had always been expected. Tasks were completed, conversations were held, and commitments were honored in a manner that reinforced the appearance of reliability. In social settings, engagement remained appropriate and composed, allowing interactions to proceed without interruption or concern. The structure of daily life did not break or collapse; instead, it persisted with a familiar sense of order that gave others confidence in what they saw and experienced through interaction.

Beneath this consistency, however, there existed a separate internal rhythm that did not align with outward expression. While external performance remained strong and dependable, internal stability carried fluctuations that were not visible in ordinary observation. Thoughts and emotions moved in patterns that were not always reflected in behavior, creating a separation between what was experienced privately and what was presented publicly. "Man looketh on the outward appearance, but the Lord looketh on the heart." (1 Samuel 16:7).

Over time, this separation developed into a quiet duality of experience. On one level, life moved forward with calm assurance, fulfilling expectations and maintaining order. On another level, there was a private awareness of unrest that did not interfere with outward function, yet remained present beneath it. This dual experience did not create immediate disruption, but it introduced a subtle tension between appearance and reality, where the surface of life remained composed while something unspoken continued to develop underneath.

The Emotional Overflow

There are moments in human experience when what has been quietly stored within begins to reveal itself through reactions that seem larger than the situation that triggered them. These moments often arrive without warning, yet they carry meaning that reaches far beyond the immediate event. What appears as a response to something small is often the expression of something much larger that has been building in silence over time. In such seasons, emotional life begins to surface in ways that feel unfamiliar, as though the inner world is speaking through the smallest openings available.

When Small Things Feel Larger Than They Are

Situations that would normally pass without attention begin to carry unexpected emotional weight. A simple conversation, a minor misunderstanding, or an ordinary delay can evoke responses that feel disproportionate to the moment itself. There is a sense that the reaction is not fully connected to what is happening externally, yet it still arises with intensity. This creates confusion within, as the mind tries to reconcile the scale of the response with the simplicity of the situation that prompted it.

Alongside this shift, irritation begins to appear in places where calmness once existed. It does not always have a clear source or identifiable cause, yet it surfaces in daily interactions with increasing frequency. Emotional sensitivity becomes heightened, where tone, timing, and even small expressions from others are perceived with greater intensity than before. The internal space begins to feel more reactive, as though it is carrying more than it can comfortably hold, even while outward life continues in its usual rhythm.

This pattern reveals an internal condition where emotional capacity has been gradually filled beyond its quiet threshold. What once remained contained within begins to move outward in subtle expressions, not because of a single event, but because of accumulated weight over time. The internal reservoir, already full from unseen layers of thought and memory, begins to influence present reactions in ways that are not always immediately understood. In this unfolding awareness, it becomes clear that emotional overflow is not sudden in origin, but the result of what has been carried silently for far longer than it appears.

The Breaking Awareness

A quiet moment arrives in a life that has been running fast for a long time. It does not announce itself with noise or drama. It comes as a gentle interruption inside ordinary routines, as though the soul pauses for a brief second and begins to observe what the mind has been ignoring for years. The surroundings remain familiar, responsibilities continue, conversations carry on, yet something within begins to ask questions that were never asked before. The heart starts noticing its own condition with a new kind of honesty that feels both unfamiliar and deeply necessary.

Something Is Not Aligned

The first honest reflection often begins in a place of silence after activity, when external demands temporarily loosen their grip. A person who has long maintained strength in front of others begins to sense a different reality within. Success still exists, duties are still fulfilled, and outward life still appears stable, yet an inner awareness begins to surface that something essential is missing. The soul recognizes that achievement alone has not produced rest, and accomplishment has not created the peace that was expected. In this realization, a deeper inquiry begins to form, one that shifts attention from outward performance toward inward condition.

A growing sensitivity develops toward the contrast between appearance and inner experience. Moments that once passed unnoticed now carry meaning. A simple pause in the day, a quiet evening, or a moment of stillness becomes a mirror revealing what busyness had previously concealed. The heart begins to recognize that emotional unrest has been present for longer than admitted, and that the absence of peace has been quietly influencing thoughts, reactions, and inner responses. This awareness does not arrive with accusation but with clarity, opening space for reflection that had been delayed for far too long.

In this awakening, the mind begins to search for understanding beyond natural explanations. Questions about peace, emotional weight, and inner stability begin to rise with sincerity. The Scripture brings light into this inner moment, reminding the heart of a deeper promise: "The peace of God, which passeth all understanding, shall keep your hearts and minds." (Philippians 4:7). This truth begins to stand as a contrast against lived experience, inviting the soul to consider whether peace is meant to be discovered in circumstances or received in a deeper place within the human spirit.

The Defining Line

A moment arrives when inner awareness gathers into a single clear recognition that can no longer be softened or postponed. Life continues in its familiar structure, responsibilities remain intact, and outward expression still carries composure, yet something within reaches a point of undeniable clarity. The contradiction between appearance and experience becomes impossible to ignore. The mind observes what the heart has carried quietly for a long time, and in that observation a truth emerges with quiet force. Everything looks intact on the surface, yet nothing feels whole within.

In this realization, the person begins to understand that emotional fracture does not always announce itself through collapse. It often exists beneath functioning days, beneath polite conversations, beneath disciplined routines that appear stable to others. The internal world carries a different story, one marked by tension that has no visible source, by heaviness that has no external explanation, and by a quiet disconnect that words struggle to describe. The outer life continues to move forward while the inner life begins to reveal that it has been carrying weight far longer than acknowledged.

This moment becomes the threshold of a deeper understanding that will guide everything that follows. It opens the way toward recognizing how unseen emotional burdens begin to shape thoughts, reactions, and even physical experience. It prepares the heart to explore how bitterness forms quietly in the background of unresolved pain, and how what remains unspoken eventually begins to influence the entire inner world. The central message of this journey begins to take shape here, that hidden emotional wounds do not remain isolated, but gradually affect the whole person in ways that reach far beyond memory.

The realization settles gently but firmly: nothing appears wrong in the external sense, yet everything within carries signs of imbalance that can no longer be dismissed. This is the doorway into deeper reflection, where the unseen layers of human experience begin to surface and demand understanding. The Scripture speaks into this inner awakening with quiet authority, reminding the heart that true alignment begins beyond outward appearance and enters into the deeper place where life is examined in truth. From this point, the journey moves forward into the hidden roots of emotional pain and the unseen formation of bitterness that shapes the human experience from within.

Chapter 2: The Offense That Stayed

In 1846, in Vienna General Hospital (Allgemeines Krankenhaus), a young Hungarian physician named **Ignaz Semmelweis** made a discovery that would later change modern medicine. At that time, he was working in the maternity ward, where two clinics operated side by side. One was staffed by doctors and medical students, and the other by midwives. What disturbed Semmelweis was a consistent and tragic pattern: women giving birth in the doctors' clinic were dying from what was called "childbed fever" at dramatically higher rates than those attended by midwives.

In 1847, Semmelweis observed something critical. Doctors were performing autopsies in the morning and then delivering babies immediately afterward without proper handwashing. He introduced a strict handwashing protocol using chlorinated lime solutions. The results were immediate and measurable: mortality rates in the doctors' clinic dropped dramatically within months. What had been silently killing hundreds of women each year was no longer spreading through invisible contamination carried on unclean hands.

But the deeper resistance did not come from bacteria or medical ignorance alone. It came from pride, disbelief, and emotional resistance within the medical community itself. Many physicians rejected Semmelweis's conclusions, not because the evidence was unclear, but because accepting it meant confronting their own responsibility in causing harm. His discovery was dismissed, and in frustration and isolation, Semmelweis experienced severe emotional distress. Historical records suggest his mental health deteriorated significantly in the final years of his life, and he died in 1865 in an asylum in Vienna, at the age of 47.

Only years later, after the development of germ theory by Louis Pasteur and Joseph Lister in the 1860s and 1870s, did Semmelweis's findings receive proper recognition. The simple act of cleansing hands before medical procedures became one of the most important transformations in medical history, saving millions of lives worldwide. What was once resisted became foundational to modern healthcare.

This story is not only about infection control. It reveals something deeper about human resistance—how truth can be seen, yet not accepted when it requires internal adjustment. Semmelweis himself is often described in historical accounts as a man deeply affected by rejection and professional isolation. His inability to find acceptance for what he knew to be true contributed to significant emotional suffering, which modern readers often interpret through the lens of unresolved internal distress.

What makes this relevant to the human experience of offense is not the medical breakthrough itself, but the pattern it reveals. Harm is not always only in the event; sometimes it continues in the refusal to release what the event has created internally. In Semmelweis's world, contamination was physical. In human emotional life, contamination is often psychological—carried through repeated thought, unresolved interpretation, and internal resistance.

The second chapter begins here: in the moment where offense does not simply happen, but remains. It becomes part of internal processing long after the event has ended. Just as invisible particles once spread infection in hospitals before they were understood, unresolved emotional injury continues to influence perception, behavior, and even physical well-being when it is not released.

Semmelweis's story reminds us that what is not cleaned—whether on hands or in the heart—does not remain neutral. It continues to act, quietly shaping outcomes until it is addressed.

The Moment That Changed Everything

There are certain experiences in life that arrive without warning and yet leave a permanent mark on the inner world. They do not always appear dramatic from the outside, and others may even continue as if nothing significant has occurred. But within the person who experiences them, something shifts in a way that is difficult to describe and impossible to ignore. A sense of trust that once felt natural begins to feel questioned, and the inner stability that was taken for granted begins to lose its quiet strength.

It may come through betrayal from someone who was once trusted without hesitation. It may arrive through rejection that feels unexpected and deeply personal. It may appear as an act of injustice where fairness was expected, or a moment of disappointment where hope had quietly taken root. Whatever the form, the impact remains similar in its emotional weight. There is a sudden realization that what was assumed to be secure has been disturbed in a way that cannot be undone by explanation alone.

In that moment, the mind often struggles to accept what has happened. There is an internal pause, as if consciousness itself is trying to catch up with the reality of the experience. The thought repeats quietly within the heart, almost in disbelief, that this should not have happened. Not because life promised perfection, but because something within expected a different outcome based on trust, relationship, or understanding. That inner expectation collides with reality, and in that collision, emotional injury begins to form its first imprint.

Even when words are spoken later, or when time begins to pass, the internal echo of that moment remains. It becomes a reference point that the heart returns to without conscious invitation. The memory does not stay as a neutral record of the past, but begins to carry emotional weight each time it is revisited. In this quiet way, the seed of deeper emotional disturbance enters the memory, marking the beginning of something that will continue to unfold within the unseen layers of the human heart.

The First Emotional Shockwave

The human mind often believes it will respond to difficult moments with clarity and control. There is an assumption that understanding will arrive quickly, that explanation will restore balance, and that reason will bring the inner world back into order. Yet when a deep emotional wound occurs, the first response is rarely organized thought. It is something far more immediate, something that rises from within before interpretation begins.

Confusion, Disbelief, Emotional Paralysis

In the aftermath of a painful moment, there is often a period where the inner world feels suspended. Thoughts do not form easily, and even simple reflection feels delayed. The mind circles the event repeatedly, as if trying to locate a missing detail that would make it acceptable or understandable. There is disbelief, not always spoken outwardly, but deeply felt within the silence of personal awareness. The reality of what has happened does not settle comfortably, and for a brief period, emotional movement feels slowed, as though the inner self is waiting for the situation to correct itself.

During this phase, even ordinary actions can feel distant. Conversations continue, responsibilities remain, yet internally there is a sense of separation from normal engagement. It is not that life stops, but that the inner experience of life becomes temporarily disconnected from the outer flow of events. This is the beginning of emotional shock, where the heart experiences something faster than the mind can fully explain.

Attempt to Understand What Just Happened

After the initial impact, the mind begins its effort to reconstruct meaning. It replays the moment, examines the sequence, and searches for logic that can reduce the emotional weight. Questions begin to form quietly within: how did this happen, why did it unfold this way, what was missed, what could have been different. This search for understanding is natural, yet it often takes place while the emotional system is still active and unsettled.

In this stage, the heart already carries the emotional imprint of the event, while the mind continues to process it analytically. There is a subtle separation between feeling and reasoning. The emotional experience has already been recorded internally, but the mind is still trying to interpret it as if it were incomplete information. This creates tension within the inner world, because explanation arrives after impact rather than before it.

Early Emotional Injury Forms

As this internal processing continues, something begins to settle deeper than thought. The emotional experience becomes structured within memory, not as a passing moment, but as an event with lasting significance. It begins to carry emotional association, meaning, and sensitivity. What was once a single experience starts to develop into an internal reference point that can be reactivated by thought or reminder.

At this stage, emotional injury is no longer just about what happened externally. It becomes about how the event is now held within. The heart begins to store the experience with emotional weight attached to it, even while the mind continues to search for understanding. This is how early internal wounds begin to form, quietly shaping perception without immediate awareness.

Mind Tries to Rationalize What Heart Already Felt

Eventually, the mind attempts to regain control by constructing explanations. It seeks reasons, patterns, and justifications that can make the experience feel manageable. Yet the emotional reality has already been registered. The heart has responded before logic arrived, and that response remains unchanged by later analysis. This creates an inner divide between what is understood intellectually and what is felt emotionally.

In this space, reasoning becomes an attempt to follow what the heart has already concluded in experience. The emotional system has reacted first, and the mind is now trying to interpret what has already been internally defined. This is where the earliest form of emotional tension stabilizes, as feeling and understanding begin to move at different speeds within the same person.

The Replay Begins

There are experiences that do not remain confined to the moment in which they occurred. Instead, they begin to return again and again within the inner world, as if the mind has developed a silent habit of revisiting what the heart has already recorded. Time moves forward in daily life, yet inside the memory continues to open the same door repeatedly, bringing the same emotional atmosphere back into awareness.

The Mind Revisits the Event Repeatedly

After the initial shock settles, the mind begins to circle back to the experience without conscious invitation. It appears during ordinary activities, in brief pauses of thought, and in moments when attention is not fully occupied. The event returns not as a complete story, but as fragments that carry emotional weight. Each return strengthens familiarity with the memory, even when the intention is to move forward.

What was once a single occurrence begins to take on a recurring presence within thought life. The mind does not simply remember it; it reenters it. This repetition slowly reshapes the way the event is held internally, giving it a continuing influence over emotional perception.

Conversations Are Replayed Word by Word

One of the most subtle forms of this replay occurs in the return of spoken words. Conversations are reconstructed internally with careful attention to tone, timing, and meaning. The mind replays not only what was said, but how it was said, often slowing moments down to examine them more closely than they were originally experienced.

In this process, language becomes emotionally charged again. Words that passed quickly in real time now carry extended reflection. The heart responds once more to what has already occurred, as if the moment is being lived again within imagination. This internal replay creates a loop where memory is no longer passive, but active and emotionally engaging.

Imagined Better Responses Begin Forming

Alongside the replay, another layer begins to develop within thought. The mind starts constructing alternative versions of the same moment. It imagines different responses, clearer words, stronger boundaries, or more effective reactions. These imagined revisions often carry a sense of correction, as if the mind is attempting to rewrite what was experienced.

Yet these internal revisions do not change the original event. Instead, they deepen engagement with it. The emotional system continues to interact with a moment that has already passed, giving it continued relevance in the present. This creates a subtle continuation of emotional involvement long after the situation has ended externally.

Sleep and Quiet Moments Trigger Repetition

In moments of rest, silence, or reduced external activity, the replay becomes even more noticeable. When distractions decrease, the mind naturally returns to unresolved emotional material. At night, or during quiet reflection, the memory can surface with renewed clarity, bringing the emotional atmosphere of the original moment back into awareness.

These quiet intervals often become spaces where the event is revisited most vividly. Without external interruption, the internal world gives full attention to what remains unresolved. In this way, silence does not always bring rest; sometimes it becomes the environment where emotional memory becomes most active.

Key Shift: The Event Is No Longer Past Tense Emotionally

At this stage, something important changes within the inner experience. Although time has moved forward externally, the emotional experience of the event continues to live in the present within memory. It is no longer held as something that happened and ended, but as something that still carries influence in current thought and feeling.

The heart continues to respond to what the mind keeps replaying, and in this ongoing cycle, the boundary between past and present begins to blur. The event remains active within emotional awareness, shaping perception as though it is still unfolding internally rather than remaining behind in time.

The Inner Argument

There comes a stage in emotional experience where memory no longer remains as simple replay. It begins to evolve into dialogue, as if the mind has created a private space where conversations continue long after the real moment has ended. This inner space is not silent in meaning, even though it is silent in sound. Within it, words are exchanged again, responses are formed, and meaning is continuously reexamined.

Internal Arguments With the Person or Situation

In this phase, the heart begins to engage in unseen dialogue with the source of the offense. The person or situation is no longer only remembered; it is mentally addressed. Arguments form inwardly, where questions are raised and responses are constructed without the presence of the other party. These internal exchanges feel real in emotion, even though they exist only within thought.

The mind attempts to complete what it believes was unfinished. It reopens the moment, not as observation, but as participation. In doing so, it gives voice to what was not expressed at the time, and it constructs replies that feel justified within the emotional framework of the memory.

Imagined Confrontations

Alongside these internal arguments, imagined confrontations begin to form. The mind creates scenarios where the situation is revisited under different conditions. Words are spoken more clearly, boundaries are expressed more firmly, and emotional balance is restored within the imagined exchange. These constructed moments provide a sense of inner correction, even though they remain entirely within thought.

In these imagined confrontations, the emotional self seeks resolution through expression. What could not be said in reality is now spoken freely in the inner world. The heart uses imagination as a space to release what remains unspoken, while still remaining connected to the original event.

Rewriting of the Past in the Mind

As this process continues, the memory itself begins to shift subtly. The mind revisits the sequence of events and adjusts interpretation. It considers alternative meanings, different intentions, and revised understandings. The past is not changed in reality, yet it is continuously reexamined in perception.

This mental rewriting does not erase the original experience. Instead, it layers interpretation upon memory, adding emotional commentary that becomes part of how the event is remembered. Over time, the memory becomes a combination of what happened and what the mind continues to add to it.

Emotional Self-Justification Begins

Within these internal dialogues, the emotional self begins to develop justification for its responses. Feelings of hurt, disappointment, or anger are given reasoning within the mind. The inner world begins to explain itself to itself, seeking validation for emotional reactions that remain active.

This justification does not always appear as conscious decision. It often forms naturally as part of internal processing. The mind seeks coherence between emotion and meaning, and in doing so, it builds explanations that support the emotional experience rather than release it.

Psychological Layer: The Mind Builds an Internal Courtroom

At this stage, the inner world takes on the structure of a courtroom within thought. The event is placed under constant review, the situation is repeatedly examined, and internal arguments continue without resolution. The mind acts as both observer and participant, presenting evidence, forming judgments, and revisiting testimony from memory.

In this internal courtroom, the emotional experience is continuously evaluated, yet never fully concluded. The heart remains engaged in ongoing interpretation, while the memory remains active as a case that is never fully closed.

The Birth of Resentment

There is a stage in emotional experience where pain begins to lose its fluid form and starts becoming structured within thought. What was once a raw reaction slowly settles into something more organized, more stable, and more persistent. The memory of the offense no longer appears as a single event, but as a reference point that begins to influence interpretation of new experiences. In psychological studies of betrayal trauma, this stage is identified as the moment when emotional memory becomes cognitively reinforced through repetition and meaning-making.[1]

In real documented clinical observations, individuals who experience interpersonal betrayal often report a gradual shift in perception toward the source of injury. Trust does not disappear instantly; it erodes through repeated internal reinforcement of the memory. The mind begins to associate the person or situation not only with the event itself, but with a pattern of expectation. Over time, even neutral interactions are filtered through the emotional imprint of the original wound. This is how perception becomes shaped without conscious awareness.

In one widely documented case study from psychological research on relational trauma, a participant described how a single incident of professional betrayal altered every future interaction with authority figures. The event itself lasted minutes, yet its emotional influence extended for years, gradually changing the way trust was experienced in all hierarchical relationships. The researchers observed that the emotional response transitioned from acute hurt into a stable cognitive-emotional framework that influenced decision-making and relational distance.[2]

This is the moment where trust begins to weaken quietly. It does not collapse suddenly; it retracts slowly. The heart begins to evaluate people and situations through a protective lens formed by memory. Even when outward behavior remains unchanged, internal openness begins to reduce. The emotional system learns to anticipate repetition of harm, and in doing so, begins to withdraw from vulnerability. What was once openness becomes guarded awareness.

At the same time, emotional distance begins to form. This distance is not always expressed outwardly. It often exists internally as reduced emotional accessibility. Conversations continue, relationships function, and responsibilities remain intact, yet the inner world no longer engages

---

[1] Jennifer J. Freyd, "Betrayal Trauma Theory," *Journal of Trauma & Dissociation* 8, no. 1 (2007): 1–13.

[2] Bessel van der Kolk, *The Body Keeps the Score: Brain, Mind, and Body in the Healing of Trauma* (New York: Viking, 2014), 86–102.

with the same depth. The emotional self begins to conserve itself, avoiding full exposure to situations that resemble past injury.

In this transition, resentment begins to take shape. It is not yet expressed hostility; it is structured emotional memory reinforced by interpretation. Psychological research identifies resentment as a sustained emotional response that arises when perceived injustice is repeatedly rehearsed internally without resolution.[3] The offense is no longer an isolated event; it becomes an active internal reference that continues to shape emotional reaction.

Spiritual reflection across multiple traditions has long recognized this internal process in symbolic language. What is not released becomes rooted within the inner life, gradually shaping perception, response, and relational openness. The emotional world begins to organize itself around unresolved experience, and what was once a moment becomes a structure within the heart.

Identity Begins to Shift

There is a subtle but profound transition in human emotional life when an event stops being something that happened and begins becoming something that defines perception itself. At first, the experience is held as a memory with emotional weight, but over time it begins to reorganize the way the inner world interprets new situations. What was once a specific moment starts influencing general expectations about people, relationships, and life itself.

"What Happened to Me" Becomes "What Life Is Like"

In the early stages of emotional injury, the mind still distinguishes between the event and life as a whole. There is still a sense that what occurred was specific, isolated, and limited to a particular circumstance. Yet as the memory is repeatedly revisited and emotionally reinforced, the interpretation begins to expand. The language of the inner world slowly shifts from describing an experience to defining reality. Instead of saying something happened, the heart begins to assume that this is how life operates.

This shift does not occur through a single decision. It develops gradually through repeated emotional recall and interpretation. Each time the memory is activated, it strengthens the association between experience and expectation. Over time, the event becomes less of a reference and more of a framework through which other experiences are measured.

Emotional Experience Begins Shaping Identity

---

[3] John W. Pennebaker and Laura A. Harber, "A Social Stage Model of Collective Coping," *Journal of Social Issues* 49, no. 4 (1993): 125–145.

As this internal restructuring continues, emotional experience begins to influence identity formation. The individual no longer relates to the event as something external to self-understanding. Instead, it becomes integrated into how the self is perceived. The inner narrative begins to absorb the emotional tone of the experience, and identity starts to reflect the accumulated emotional interpretation of past events.

Psychological research in trauma studies has shown that repeated emotional activation of unresolved experiences can contribute to identity-based perception shifts, where individuals begin to interpret new experiences through the lens of prior emotional injury.[4] This does not mean identity is replaced, but rather that perception becomes filtered through emotional memory.

Subtle Victim Awareness Forms

At this stage, a quiet form of self-awareness begins to develop, shaped by accumulated emotional interpretation. It is not always conscious or openly expressed, but it influences internal dialogue and expectation. The mind begins to anticipate similar outcomes in future interactions, and this anticipation becomes part of how situations are emotionally processed.

This awareness is subtle because it often exists beneath language. It is not necessarily spoken as identity, but it is felt as expectation. Over time, this expectation influences interpretation of new experiences, reinforcing the internal framework that has been formed through repetition of emotional memory.

Emotional Guarding Begins

As perception becomes increasingly shaped by past emotional experience, the inner world begins to adopt protective positioning. Emotional openness is gradually reduced in situations that resemble previous injury. This guarding is not always intentional; it develops as an adaptive response to perceived emotional risk.

Trust, once given freely, becomes measured and cautious. Engagement with people and situations begins to carry an internal filter shaped by prior emotional outcomes. While outward interaction may remain unchanged, the inner experience of interaction becomes more restrained, selective, and self-protective.

Key Transformation: Experience Becomes Personality Filter

At this point, a significant internal transformation occurs. The emotional experience no longer functions as an isolated memory. It becomes a lens through which perception is filtered. This means that

---

[4] Bessel van der Kolk, *The Body Keeps the Score: Brain, Mind, and Body in the Healing of Trauma* (New York: Viking, 2014), 93.

new experiences are no longer encountered in isolation; they are interpreted through the emotional structure formed by past injury.

What was once an event becomes an interpretive framework. The heart begins to respond not only to what is happening, but to what similar experiences have previously meant. In this way, emotional memory begins to shape personality expression, influencing how situations are understood, how relationships are approached, and how trust is internally managed.

The Quiet Weight of Memory

Human life continues forward through schedules, conversations, responsibilities, and expectations, yet within the inner world another layer begins to operate quietly. Memory begins to carry emotional charge that does not fade with time. Certain moments return without invitation, especially during silence or rest, and they bring the same emotional intensity as the original experience. The heart begins to hold a background pressure that shapes perception without announcing itself.

There are individuals whose lives demonstrate this reality with unusual clarity. Nelson Mandela, during his years of imprisonment on Robben Island, described how certain memories of injustice and separation would return with striking emotional clarity even in ordinary moments of routine labor. In those reflections, he noted that physical confinement created space for deep internal processing, where past events repeatedly surfaced with emotional force that time alone did not dissolve. His writings reveal that memory can remain active long after the external event has ended, shaping inner endurance and emotional awareness in quiet but persistent ways.[5]

This pattern reveals a deeper truth about human experience. Stored emotional pain does not remain dormant; it interacts with daily life in subtle ways. A word, a silence, or a passing thought can activate a full emotional response that seems larger than the present moment. Over time, this creates a sense of internal fatigue, as though the mind is continuously carrying more than the visible world requires. The external life remains structured, yet the internal atmosphere carries a weight that influences interpretation, reaction, and emotional availability.

Within this state, spiritual awareness begins to surface in a different form. The soul recognizes that unresolved emotional material does not remain silent within the human experience. It continues to speak through mood, memory, and interpretation of present events. The quiet weight of memory becomes a companion that shapes how life is felt, even when life appears unchanged on the surface.

---

[5] Nelson Mandela, *Long Walk to Freedom: The Autobiography of Nelson Mandela* (Boston: Little, Brown and Company, 1994), 487.

The Locked Door

This final movement within the chapter brings the inner journey into a moment of clear recognition. What began as an event in time now appears as something that has taken shape within the inner structure of thought and emotion. The reader stands at a threshold where experience becomes understanding, and memory becomes formation. The heart begins to perceive that certain moments do not remain external stories, but settle into the architecture of inner life, influencing perception, response, and expectation in a continuous way.

The Emotional Turning Point

At this stage of awareness, a quiet realization emerges that the earlier offense has established residence within memory and continues to influence present emotional experience. The mind recognizes patterns of return, where the same moment reappears in thought with consistent emotional weight, shaping interpretation of new experiences through the lens of what was once endured. Within psychological study of emotional memory, scholars such as Bessel van der Kolk describe how the human system retains lived emotional experiences in both narrative and physiological form, allowing past events to remain active within present awareness and influence perception and behavior over time.[6]

From this recognition arises the central direction of the entire chapter. Bitterness begins forming at the point where emotional pain receives preservation within inner dialogue rather than transformation through release and understanding. What is preserved continues to shape interpretation, and what continues to shape interpretation begins to form identity. The inner world gradually organizes itself around the memory of the offense, allowing it to become a reference point for trust, expectation, and emotional engagement with life.

This chapter concludes within a space of awareness rather than closure. The reader stands within the understanding that internal captivity often develops quietly, through repetition of thought and continuity of emotional preservation. The next movement of the book opens into deeper exploration of how the human spirit responds when memory becomes structure and when structure begins to influence the entire experience of living.

---

[6] Bessel van der Kolk, *The Body Keeps the Score: Brain, Mind, and Body in the Healing of Trauma* (New York: Viking, 2014), 214.

Chapter 3: Bitterness Takes Root

On April 4, 1968, in Memphis, Tennessee, the assassination of Dr. Martin Luther King Jr. sent shockwaves across the United States and the world. He was only 39 years old when he was shot at the Lorraine Motel. The public response was immediate: grief, outrage, confusion, and fear. But beyond the public mourning, something more personal unfolded in the lives of those closest to the civil rights movement—the people who had worked, suffered, and sacrificed alongside him.

One of the most documented responses in the aftermath came from Coretta Scott King, his wife. In the days following his death, she publicly continued his message of nonviolence and restraint, even while personally experiencing deep emotional devastation. In interviews and public addresses over the years, she often reflected on how grief, anger, and emotional burden could either harden into long-term internal pain or be transformed into purpose and continuation of meaning.

In the broader civil rights community, however, not everyone processed the event in the same way. Many activists and supporters experienced what psychologists later describe as prolonged grief and moral injury—the internal struggle that arises when a deeply meaningful life is violently interrupted. For some, the unresolved emotional impact of King's assassination contributed to long-term stress, distrust, and emotional exhaustion in their continued activism. Historical accounts and psychological studies of civil rights workers in the late 1960s and 1970s describe elevated levels of burnout, depression, and chronic emotional strain among those who remained deeply immersed in the movement after his death.

At the same time, Coretta Scott King chose a different internal direction. Instead of allowing the assassination to define her life through bitterness, she devoted herself to continuing the work of nonviolence through the Martin Luther King Jr. Center for Nonviolent Social Change, which she helped establish in 1968. Her public stance consistently emphasized that hatred and retaliation would not be the final response to violence. While she never denied the pain or injustice of her husband's death, she refused to let it become the defining structure of her internal world.

This contrast reveals something important about human emotional life. The same event can enter different people's inner worlds and produce different long-term outcomes. In one direction, pain can remain active and begin to structure perception, memory, and emotional response. In another direction, pain can be acknowledged but prevented from becoming the organizing principle of identity. What determines the difference is not the severity of the event, but the internal response to it over time.

Bitterness does not usually begin as bitterness. It begins as justified pain. It begins as memory that has not been processed beyond its original intensity. But when that memory is repeatedly revisited without release, it begins to settle into a deeper layer of emotional life. It stops being an event and starts becoming a state. At that point, the person is no longer simply remembering what happened—they are living inside the emotional residue of it.

This is where the third chapter begins. Not at the moment of injury itself, but at the point where injury begins to take root inside the human system and quietly reshape how life is experienced from within.

The Inner Conversation Begins

At this stage of the human experience, the silence within the mind begins to change its nature. What once felt like a passing memory now begins to return with structure, rhythm, and interpretation. The offense is no longer a single moment recalled occasionally; it becomes a repeated internal conversation that arises without invitation. The mind begins to speak to itself about what happened, revisiting the event not as history, but as ongoing commentary. In this quiet repetition, emotional experience begins to take shape in language, and language begins to shape emotional reality.

Within this unfolding internal movement, justification begins to appear gently and almost unnoticed. The heart begins to construct meaning around the pain, and that meaning slowly becomes supportive of the emotion itself. Thoughts arise that affirm the inner reaction, reinforcing the sense that what was felt was appropriate, understandable, and deserved. In this space, the mind begins to defend what the heart experienced, as though protecting the wound ensures its validity. Over time, this defense becomes familiar, and familiarity begins to feel like truth.

"I was right to feel this way" begins to echo internally, not as a single thought, but as a repeated tone within the mind. It becomes part of the emotional rhythm of reflection, surfacing during quiet moments, returning during pauses in activity, and appearing in the spaces between daily responsibilities. Memory no longer functions as observation alone;

it becomes a dialogue partner that reinforces emotional interpretation. The offense is no longer something remembered; it becomes something discussed inwardly, as though still unfolding.

As this process continues, emotional reasoning begins to replace emotional processing. Instead of releasing the experience, the mind analyzes it, revisits it, and reconstructs it in different forms. Each reconstruction carries emotional weight, and each emotional weight strengthens the internal narrative. The mind begins to build coherence around the pain rather than distance from it. In this way, thought becomes a container for emotion, and repetition becomes the mechanism through which emotional meaning is preserved.

Psychologically, this marks a significant transition within the inner life of a person. The mind begins to defend the wound instead of releasing it, and in doing so, it assigns value to the continued presence of the injury. What was once a reaction begins to develop structure, and what develops structure begins to influence perception. The inner world starts organizing itself around the remembered offense, allowing it to occupy space within ongoing thought patterns.

From a spiritual perspective, a subtle but profound principle becomes visible. Agreement with pain strengthens its authority within the heart. When the mind repeatedly returns to the same emotional justification, it creates internal alignment with the experience of hurt. This alignment gives the emotion continuity, allowing it to remain active within the inner life. What is repeatedly affirmed begins to feel established, and what feels established begins to guide emotional interpretation of present and future experiences.

Thus, the inner conversation becomes more than thought. It becomes a shaping force, quietly influencing how life is felt, understood, and remembered.

The Logic of Anger

As the inner conversation continues to develop, emotion begins to move from raw experience into structured reasoning. Anger, which once emerged as an immediate response to pain, slowly begins to feel organized, coherent, and even justified. It no longer appears as a sudden emotional wave, but as a carefully constructed interpretation of what has been endured. The mind starts to give shape to the intensity, and in doing so, it builds an internal framework that supports the persistence of the feeling.

Within this framework, explanations begin to form naturally. The mind returns to the event and reconstructs it repeatedly, each time adding clarity that reinforces the emotional stance. What was once confusing begins to feel understandable, and what was understandable begins to feel morally supported. Every recall strengthens the sense that the emotional response was appropriate to the situation. In this process, anger begins to feel less like reaction and more like conclusion.

Each repetition of memory adds weight to the internal argument. The mind does not simply revisit the offense; it evaluates it, measures it, and interprets it through a growing sense of fairness. The emotional intensity becomes tied to reasoning, and reasoning begins to sustain emotional intensity. Over time, the feeling of anger becomes structured enough that it no longer requires external confirmation. It begins to validate itself through repetition alone.

At this stage, external validation loses its importance. The inner world no longer depends on outside perspectives to confirm emotional truth. The repeated internal narrative becomes sufficient evidence for the heart. The emotional position becomes stable within itself, reinforced by continuous reflection. What others might say or not say no longer carries the same weight, because the mind has already constructed its conclusion.

In this transformation, emotional experience begins to shift in nature. What was once a reaction to pain begins to feel like truth about reality. The emotion is no longer questioned from within; instead, it is defended as accurate interpretation of what occurred. The boundary between feeling and fact becomes less distinct in the inner world, allowing anger to take on the appearance of clarity rather than response.

Psychologically, this stage reflects the consolidation of emotional interpretation into cognitive structure. The mind strengthens its own reasoning loops, creating stability around emotional conclusions that originated in pain.

From a documented clinical perspective, research on emotional memory and cognitive reinforcement shows that repeated recall of emotionally charged events strengthens belief certainty associated with those memories, especially when the memory is repeatedly rehearsed without corrective emotional processing.[7] This aligns with the observed pattern in which anger becomes increasingly structured and self-reinforcing over time.

The Shift From Hurt to Identity

As the internal dialogue deepens and the logic of emotion becomes more established, something subtle yet profound begins to occur within the human inner world. The experience that once belonged to a moment in time begins to lose its separation from the self. What was once

[7] Elizabeth F. Loftus, "Planting Misleading Information into Memory," *Journal of Cognitive Neuroscience* 12, no. 4 (2000): 590.

"something that happened" starts to feel like something that belongs within the structure of who a person is. The boundary between experience and identity begins to soften, and emotional memory begins to settle into the deeper layers of self-perception.

At this stage, language within the inner narrative begins to shift in a quiet but significant way. The mind no longer speaks only about the event; it begins to speak from within it. Instead of describing an experience, it begins to define the self through it. The phrase "what happened" slowly gives way to an internal sense of "what defines me." This transformation does not occur through deliberate decision, but through repeated reflection that gradually shapes emotional understanding into identity formation.

As this shift continues, emotional memory begins to function as a filter through which all perception is processed. New experiences are unconsciously interpreted through the lens of the remembered wound. Interactions, decisions, and interpretations begin to carry the imprint of the past offense, even when the present moment contains no direct connection to it. The emotional memory becomes a background framework that influences how reality is understood and felt.

Self perception begins adjusting around this internal structure. The individual no longer simply remembers what happened; the individual begins to interpret themselves through what happened. In this way, identity begins to form around emotional residue. The inner narrative no longer separates experience from selfhood with clarity, and over time, the distinction between the two becomes increasingly difficult to recognize within personal reflection.

Psychologically, this reflects a well observed process in which repeated emotional recall contributes to identity consolidation around significant experiences. When emotional memory is reinforced without resolution, it begins to function as a stable reference point for self definition, shaping perception, expectation, and behavior.

From a spiritual perspective, a deeper principle becomes visible within this transformation. Identity begins where repeated thought stabilizes emotion. When a thought returns often enough to carry emotional weight consistently, it begins to form structure within the inner life. That structure gradually influences how the self is understood, not as a collection of moments, but as a continuous interpretation shaped by what is repeatedly held within the heart.

In this way, hurt moves beyond experience and quietly enters the foundation of identity itself.

Emotional Duality

As the inner structure of experience continues to evolve, a noticeable division begins to form between outward expression and inward reality. On the surface, behavior remains composed, functional, and socially appropriate. Responsibilities are carried out, conversations continue, and presence in daily life appears stable. Yet beneath this external continuity, another world begins to operate with a different emotional temperature, responding not to present events alone, but to accumulated internal material that has not been resolved.

Within this internal world, emotional reactivity becomes more immediate and less filtered. Recollections of past offenses, interpretations of present interactions, and anticipations of future disappointments begin to interact in a continuous stream of thought. The inner life carries responses that are not always visible outwardly, creating a layered existence in which emotion is experienced in one domain while expression is managed in another. Over time, this separation becomes familiar, and familiarity begins to feel normal.

Silence begins to carry greater meaning than speech during this stage. What is not said begins to hold more emotional weight than what is expressed. A pause in conversation, a lack of response, or a change in tone can activate internal interpretation that remains hidden from others. The inner world becomes highly responsive, while the outer world continues in structured calm. This contrast forms a lived duality in which meaning is constantly generated within, even when nothing outward appears to change.

Emotional control continues to function in external settings, yet within the private world, emotional turbulence persists without interruption. The individual learns to maintain appearance while simultaneously managing internal fluctuation. This does not occur as deception, but as adaptation to sustained emotional complexity. Over time, the separation between these two experiences becomes more defined, and the person begins to experience life through parallel channels of expression and emotion.

Psychologically, this stage reflects the beginning of emotional compartmentalization. Research in affect regulation describes this process as the mind's capacity to separate emotional experience from external expression, allowing functioning to continue while internal emotional processing remains active and unresolved.[8] This division often emerges when emotional material exceeds the capacity for

---

[8] James J. Gross, "Emotion Regulation: Affective, Cognitive, and Social Consequences," *Psychophysiology* 39, no. 3 (2002): 282–283.

immediate integration, leading to parallel internal and external states of experience.

At the core of this transformation lies a simple but profound reality. One life is seen, while another is lived internally. The visible self continues to operate within social structures, while the inner self carries the accumulated weight of unprocessed emotional meaning. This duality becomes the silent architecture of lived experience at this stage of the journey.

Emotional Numbness or Volatility

As the inner world continues under sustained emotional strain, it begins to express itself in contrasting patterns that reveal a deeper instability beneath outward functioning. In some individuals, emotional experience begins to diminish in intensity, as though the heart has gradually reduced its responsiveness in order to manage continuous internal pressure. In others, emotional sensitivity increases, causing even minor interactions to carry amplified meaning and reaction. These two expressions, though different in appearance, arise from the same underlying condition of accumulated and unprocessed emotional weight.

In the first pattern, emotional numbness develops as a form of internal conservation. Feelings that were once immediate and vivid begin to lose clarity, as the mind reduces emotional engagement in order to maintain stability. Life continues, yet emotional depth becomes less accessible. In the second pattern, emotional volatility emerges, where reactions become more immediate and less proportionate to external events. Small triggers activate large internal responses, often surprising even the individual experiencing them.

Within both expressions, emotional balance begins to shift. Stability that once allowed consistent interpretation of experiences becomes less predictable. The internal system struggles to regulate emotional input in a steady way, resulting in fluctuations that alternate between withdrawal and intensity. These patterns may appear different externally, yet internally they reflect the same underlying process of emotional overload that has not found resolution.

Over time, the ability to regulate emotional responses weakens gradually. This weakening does not occur suddenly, but through repeated internal strain where emotional material is carried without release or integration. The heart continues to respond, but its responses become either muted or amplified depending on internal conditions. The natural rhythm of emotional processing becomes disrupted, and equilibrium becomes increasingly difficult to maintain.

Psychologically, this stage aligns with observed patterns in affect regulation where prolonged exposure to unresolved emotional stress can lead to either blunted emotional responsiveness or heightened emotional reactivity. Both outcomes reflect a system attempting to manage overload through different adaptive strategies.

Research in trauma physiology notes that sustained emotional stress can lead to dysregulation of affective response systems, resulting in either hypoarousal or hyperarousal states depending on individual adaptation patterns.[9] This framework helps explain why emotional experience may shift toward either numbness or volatility when internal processing remains incomplete over time.

From a spiritual perspective, a consistent principle emerges. What is not healed eventually finds expression in extremes. When emotional healing is delayed, the inner life seeks release through intensified contrast, either by withdrawing feeling or amplifying it beyond proportion. In both cases, the inner world reveals that unresolved pain continues to seek expression, even when it is not consciously acknowledged.

The Root Formation

At this final point within the chapter, there is a quiet recognition that something within the inner world has shifted from movement into permanence. What once arrived as an emotional response now feels established, as though it has taken up residence within the deeper layers of thought and feeling. The offense is no longer experienced as an occasional memory that returns and fades, but as a consistent presence that influences perception even in its silence.

This awareness brings with it the understanding that the emotion has settled into structure. It no longer appears as something temporary passing through the mind, but as something integrated into the way experiences are interpreted. The internal landscape has adjusted around it, allowing it to remain present without resistance. In this stage, emotional life begins to reflect stability of pattern rather than fluctuation of reaction.

A deeper realization emerges that an internal agreement has formed with the offense. This agreement is not always conscious or deliberate, yet it becomes evident through repeated thought, sustained emotional framing, and continued internal reference. The mind has returned to the same interpretation often enough that it now feels familiar, and

---

[9] Bessel A. van der Kolk, *The Body Keeps the Score: Brain, Mind, and Body in the Healing of Trauma* (New York: Viking, 2014), 88.

familiarity has quietly become acceptance. Through this process, emotional alignment with the remembered injury begins to solidify.

As this internal alignment strengthens, emotional architecture begins to change shape. The structure of response, interpretation, and memory adjusts itself around the established emotional presence. What was once a reaction to an event becomes a framework through which other experiences are filtered. The inner world begins to organize itself around this formation, allowing it to influence perception in both subtle and continuous ways.

This moment marks a transition point into deeper reflection. The chapter does not close with resolution, but with recognition that something foundational has occurred within the human inner life. The emotional landscape has shifted into structure, and structure carries consequences that extend beyond memory into identity, perception, and spiritual awareness.

From this point forward, the exploration moves toward understanding the deeper spiritual implications of what it means when emotional pain becomes internal structure rather than passing experience.

Chapter 4: The Body Keeps the Score

On March 11, 2004, in Madrid, Spain, coordinated bombings struck commuter trains during the morning rush hour. The attacks killed 193 people and injured more than 2,000. Among the survivors was a 34-year-old office worker named **María Jesús González**, who had been traveling on one of the affected trains. She survived physically, but like many survivors of that day, she did not return to her previous state of health or emotional stability.

In the months that followed, María began experiencing persistent symptoms that medical examinations could not fully explain. She reported insomnia, sudden panic episodes, heart palpitations, and recurring intrusive memories of the explosion. Even in safe environments, her body would react as if danger were still present. Loud sounds triggered immediate physical responses. Sleep became fragmented. Her nervous system appeared to remain in a constant state of alert.

Over time, she was diagnosed with post-traumatic stress disorder. Treatment included psychological counseling and gradual exposure therapy, but recovery was slow and uneven. What stood out in her case was not only the psychological memory of the event, but the physical persistence of it. Her body seemed to continue responding to danger long after the danger had ended.

In later therapeutic sessions, María began working on processing not only the memory of the event, but the emotional meanings attached to it—fear, helplessness, and anger toward what had happened. As she gradually engaged in structured trauma therapy, including cognitive behavioral techniques and guided emotional processing, she reported a slow but noticeable change. The intensity of physical symptoms began to decrease. Sleep improved. Panic episodes became less frequent. Her body, which had remained in a prolonged stress response, started to settle.

There was no single moment where everything changed. Instead, improvement appeared in layers. First in sleep, then in physical tension, and later in emotional reactivity. What was most significant was that recovery did not come only through understanding the event, but through the gradual regulation of the body's stress response system over time. Modern trauma research has since confirmed this pattern: traumatic experiences are not stored only as memories in the mind, but as physiological imprints in the nervous system, shaping heart rate, muscle tension, hormonal balance, and reflexive responses.

In María's case, what allowed restoration was not forgetting the event, nor changing what had happened, but helping the body gradually learn that the danger was no longer present. Over time, her system stopped reacting to memory as if it were current reality. The body began to differentiate between past threat and present safety.

This is where the deeper meaning of this chapter begins. Human experience is not stored only in thought. It is carried in muscle tension, breathing patterns, sleep cycles, and stress responses. What is not resolved emotionally is often retained physically. And what is carried physically continues to influence perception long after the original event has ended.

The story of survivors like María shows that healing is not only a mental process. It is also biological. The body remembers what the mind tries to move past, and it expresses unresolved experience in physical form until that experience is gradually processed and released.

Chapter 4 begins here: at the point where suffering is no longer only a memory of the mind, but a lived condition of the body itself.

The First Physical Signals

As the internal emotional world continues under sustained pressure, the human body begins to register changes that are subtle at first, yet increasingly difficult to ignore over time. These signals do not arrive as dramatic events or sudden breakdowns. Instead, they appear as quiet variations in physical comfort, small interruptions in normal energy flow, and mild sensations that seem disconnected from any clear external cause. The body begins to communicate in ways that are indirect, yet consistent in their presence.

In the early stages, fatigue becomes noticeable even when daily activity has not significantly changed. The individual may find that ordinary routines require greater effort than before, or that recovery after rest feels incomplete. This fatigue does not always correspond to physical exertion, which creates a sense of confusion about its origin. Alongside this, there may be mild tension developing in areas such as the shoulders, head, or chest, appearing without physical injury or identifiable strain. These sensations often remain in the background of awareness, acknowledged but not fully interpreted.

Throughout the day, energy levels may begin to fluctuate in ways that feel inconsistent with external circumstances. Moments of clarity and engagement may be followed by unexpected drops in focus or physical vitality. These variations can appear without warning, creating an experience of uneven internal rhythm. Because there is no immediate external explanation, the mind often searches for practical reasons such as schedule, diet, or sleep patterns, even when these factors do not fully account for the experience.

Psychologically, this stage reflects the beginning of the nervous system registering internal load. The body begins to respond to sustained emotional activity in ways that precede full cognitive recognition. Emotional strain, especially when prolonged and unprocessed, activates physiological pathways that influence tension, energy regulation, and sensory awareness. These responses occur gradually, forming patterns that are often recognized only after they become consistent.

A key reality emerges at this stage. The body begins responding before conscious awareness fully acknowledges the issue. This means that physiological signals may appear while the mind continues to interpret life as manageable or unchanged. The separation between internal emotional activity and physical expression becomes more noticeable as the body communicates what has not yet been fully processed in thought.

From a clinical perspective, research in psychophysiology has shown that sustained emotional stress can influence autonomic nervous system regulation, leading to early physical manifestations such as muscle tension, fatigue, and altered energy regulation even before conscious emotional labeling occurs.[10] This supports the observation that the body often reflects internal states prior to full psychological recognition.

Sleep Disturbance and Inner Restlessness

As emotional pressure continues to accumulate within the inner world, one of the earliest systems to reflect this imbalance is the rhythm of rest. Sleep, which normally serves as a period of restoration and integration, begins to lose its depth and continuity. The transition into rest becomes less natural, as though the mind carries an active current that resists full disengagement from thought and emotional processing.

In this phase, entering a deep state of rest requires greater effort than before. The individual may lie down with physical exhaustion yet experience an inability to settle internally. The mind remains partially engaged, continuing patterns of reflection that were present during

---

[10] Robert M. Sapolsky, "Stress, Stress-Related Disease, and Emotional Regulation," *Annual Review of Neuroscience* 27 (2004): 101–102.

waking hours. This creates a condition where rest is approached physically, yet not fully achieved internally, producing a sense of separation between body relaxation and mental quietness.

Sleep cycles may also become fragmented. There may be frequent interruptions during the night or a pattern of early waking that breaks the continuity of restorative rest. Even when sleep occurs, it may feel light or incomplete, as though the deeper layers of restoration have not been fully accessed. Upon waking, there is often a sense that recovery has not matched the duration of rest, leaving the body and mind still carrying traces of fatigue.

During quieter hours, particularly at night, mental activity often becomes more pronounced. Without external demands or distractions, the mind begins to revisit unresolved thoughts, interpretations, and emotional impressions. This period of reduced external stimulation allows internal material to surface with greater clarity, and emotional replay may become more vivid. The absence of external noise amplifies internal dialogue, making it more noticeable within awareness.

Over time, this pattern produces a consistent sense of incomplete restoration. Even after extended periods of rest, the individual may feel that full recovery has not been achieved. This experience does not always relate to physical exertion alone, but to the ongoing internal activity that continues during supposed rest states. The body rests, yet the mind continues its processing cycles in a reduced but persistent form.

From a psychological perspective, sleep research has shown that emotional arousal and cognitive rumination can significantly influence sleep quality, particularly by disrupting the transition into deeper restorative stages of sleep and increasing nocturnal awakenings.[11] This highlights the connection between sustained emotional activity and altered rest architecture.

At a deeper level, a consistent spiritual principle becomes evident. Inner unrest does not pause when external activity stops. The absence of outward motion does not automatically translate into internal stillness. Instead, whatever remains active within thought and emotion continues its expression into the quiet hours, shaping the quality of rest itself.

Anxiety Without Clear Origin

As emotional burden continues to settle within the inner world, a new kind of experience begins to surface, one that does not always

---

[11] Harvey A. R. and Espie C. A., "Insomnia as a Mechanism of Emotional Dysregulation," *Journal of Abnormal Psychology* 120, no. 2 (2011): 428–430.

present itself with a clear story or identifiable cause. The person continues to move through daily life, yet there is a subtle sense of internal pressure that seems to exist without a specific moment of origin. It is not tied to one memory or one situation, but rather feels like a quiet undercurrent that follows awareness throughout the day. This creates an experience where life appears normal externally, while internally there is a continuous sense of unnamed tension.

In this stage, anticipation begins to color perception. The mind becomes gently alert, as though waiting for something that has not yet been defined. Ordinary environments are still familiar, yet they are now received through a more sensitive internal filter. Sounds, interactions, and even silence can feel slightly intensified within awareness, not because of their actual intensity, but because the inner system is already partially activated. This state does not always produce clear fear, yet it carries a sense of readiness that shapes how each moment is experienced.

As this condition continues, the body begins to participate in this internal atmosphere. There may be a subtle tightening in physical posture, a quiet acceleration in thought patterns, or a background sense of alertness that does not fully settle even during rest. The emotional system appears to remain partially engaged, as though it has not fully returned to a baseline of calm. Over time, this becomes less noticeable as a disruption and more recognizable as a consistent internal environment.

What makes this experience particularly significant is that it often develops without a clearly defined external trigger. The absence of an identifiable cause can itself create confusion, because the body responds as though something requires attention, while the mind struggles to locate what that "something" might be. This creates a loop where internal sensation and external interpretation do not fully align, yet the experience remains real and persistent.

From a psychological perspective, research in stress physiology has shown that sustained activation of the nervous system can persist even in the absence of immediate external threat, reflecting a state in which internal regulatory systems remain sensitized due to accumulated emotional load.[12] This helps explain how internal tension can exist as a background condition rather than a response to a single event.

At a deeper level, a consistent principle emerges. Emotion begins to function less as a reaction to life events and more as a continuous

---

[12] Robert M. Sapolsky, "Why Stress Is Bad for Your Brain," *Science* 273, no. 5276 (1996): 749–750.

physiological setting through which life is experienced. In this stage, the inner world does not simply respond to reality; it begins to shape the way reality is internally received.

Manifestation of Emotional Load

As internal emotional strain continues over time, the experience of the body begins to reflect this sustained inner condition in increasingly noticeable ways. The individual may observe that physical comfort no longer remains consistent throughout the day. Instead, different forms of bodily discomfort begin to appear in patterns that seem connected to periods of internal tension, even when no immediate external cause is present. These experiences often develop gradually, making them appear as ordinary physical fluctuations at first.

Head pressure, muscle tightness, and digestive uneasiness can emerge during or after periods of prolonged internal reflection or emotional activity. Energy levels may shift in ways that appear closely tied to mental and emotional states, where moments of increased internal agitation coincide with physical fatigue or heaviness. The body begins to reflect internal repetition of thought, as though certain emotional patterns carry a physiological echo that expresses itself through physical sensation. Over time, this creates a lived experience where emotional activity and bodily response appear increasingly interconnected.

As this condition continues, physical resilience may begin to feel less stable than before. Recovery after exertion may take longer, and the sense of steady physical vitality may fluctuate more noticeably. These changes do not necessarily indicate a single point of breakdown, but rather a gradual adjustment of the body to sustained internal load. The system appears to respond to ongoing emotional pressure by distributing it through physical channels, allowing internal tension to find expression in bodily form.

From a psychological and physiological perspective, research in stress medicine has documented how chronic emotional activation can influence multiple bodily systems, including muscular tension patterns, gastrointestinal function, and autonomic regulation, reflecting the integrated nature of emotional and physical processing in the human organism.[13] This supports the understanding that internal experience and physical condition are not isolated domains, but interconnected expressions of a unified system.

---

[13] George F. Solomon and Rudolf H. Moos, "Emotions, Stress, and Health: An Overview," in *Handbook of Stress: Theoretical and Clinical Aspects*, ed. Leo Goldberger and Shlomo Breznitz, 2nd ed. (New York: Free Press, 1993), 250.

At a deeper level, this stage reveals an important principle. The body becomes a participant in emotional experience, not merely a vessel carrying it. What is repeatedly carried in thought and feeling begins to shape physical expression, creating a lived interface between emotional memory and bodily response. In this way, internal load gradually becomes observable through the language of the body itself.

The Emotional Body Settles Into Pattern

As emotional experience continues over an extended period, the body begins to adjust itself around the consistent presence of internal pressure. What was once experienced as occasional tension gradually becomes a more familiar baseline. The system begins to function within this adjusted range, where heightened alertness or subtle strain feels increasingly normal. This shift is not sudden, but gradual, as the body learns to operate within the conditions it has repeatedly experienced.

Over time, the sense of full physical relaxation becomes less frequent. Even during moments intended for rest, there may remain a quiet residual activation within the system, as though complete internal release is not easily reached. The body appears to recalibrate its sense of balance around sustained emotional input, organizing its rhythms in response to what has been consistently carried within thought and feeling. This creates a lived experience where rest and tension exist closer together than before.

In this stage, emotional history begins to take on a physiological dimension. Repeated emotional states do not remain only in memory, but gradually influence how the body establishes its sense of normal functioning. The distinction between emotional experience and physical condition becomes less defined, as both begin to reflect the same underlying pattern of sustained internal load. The body, in its adaptive intelligence, incorporates what is repeatedly experienced into its operational rhythm.

From a physiological perspective, research in psychophysiology has shown that chronic psychological stress can lead to long term alterations in autonomic and endocrine regulation, effectively shifting baseline physiological states toward sustained activation patterns rather than temporary responses to acute events.[14] This demonstrates how persistent emotional conditions can influence the body's regulatory systems over time.

At a deeper level, this reveals a significant principle. The body does not merely respond to emotion; it organizes itself around it. What is

---

[14] Bruce S. McEwen, "Protective and Damaging Effects of Stress Mediators," *New England Journal of Medicine* 338, no. 3 (1998): 171.

repeatedly experienced internally begins to shape the rhythm of physical existence, allowing emotional history to become part of the body's ongoing biological expression.

◆ Page 15: The Integrated Realization Theme: Mind and Body Are Not Separate

At this stage of awareness, there comes a clearer recognition that emotional experience and physical condition are not operating as separate realities within human life. What is carried internally through thought, memory, and unresolved feeling begins to reveal itself in the condition of the body over time. The individual begins to see that internal states are not confined to abstract mental space, but participate in shaping physical experience in consistent and observable ways.

This realization often arrives through accumulated observation rather than sudden insight. Patterns that once appeared unrelated begin to form a coherent picture, where emotional intensity, sustained internal conflict, and periods of physical discomfort appear connected through continuity rather than coincidence. The awareness grows that the body has been responding throughout, not as a separate system, but as an integrated participant in the overall emotional life of the person.

As this understanding deepens, the earlier tendency to separate emotional experience from physical reality begins to shift. There is a movement toward integration, where the internal life is no longer viewed in isolation from its physical expression. This does not diminish the complexity of either dimension, but instead brings them into a more unified framework of understanding, where both mind and body are seen as cooperating within a single living system.

From a physiological and psychological perspective, research has demonstrated that emotional processing and bodily regulation are deeply interconnected through neuroendocrine and autonomic pathways, allowing sustained psychological states to influence physical functioning over time in measurable ways.[15] This supports the understanding that emotional life is continuously embodied rather than existing apart from physical experience.

At a deeper level, this stage opens the way toward a broader awareness of healing. When emotional and physical dimensions are understood as interconnected, the possibility of release becomes more holistic. The transition into the next chapter naturally moves toward this

---

[15] Antonio Damasio, *Descartes' Error: Emotion, Reason, and the Human Brain* (New York: Avon Books, 1994), 164.

exploration, where integration of understanding becomes the foundation for restoration.

Chapter 5: A Prison Without Bars

On June 17, 1994, in the city of Los Angeles, California, former NFL player **O. J. Simpson** was involved in an incident that would become one of the most widely publicized legal cases in American history. His former wife, **Nicole Brown Simpson**, and her friend **Ron Goldman** were found murdered outside her home in Brentwood, Los Angeles. What followed was a criminal trial beginning in 1995 that captured global attention for months, often referred to as the "Trial of the Century."

While the legal process focused on evidence, testimony, and courtroom arguments, another dimension unfolded quietly in public life: the long-term emotional impact on families connected to the victims. Nicole Brown Simpson's family, particularly her sister **Denise Brown**, spoke in interviews over the years about the ongoing psychological weight of grief and unresolved anger. The absence of closure in emotional terms meant that, even as time passed, the psychological presence of the event remained active in their daily lives.

In multiple public statements and interviews following the trial, members of Nicole Brown Simpson's family described how grief, anger, and public attention created a prolonged emotional strain. In 1997, Denise Brown founded a nonprofit organization called **Nicole Brown Charitable Foundation**, focusing on domestic violence awareness. In later reflections, she expressed that continuing to live inside anger or hatred did not bring relief, but instead prolonged emotional suffering.

Psychological studies of families affected by violent crime have repeatedly shown a pattern: when grief is combined with unresolved anger or ongoing internal re-examination of the event, individuals can experience prolonged stress responses. These may include sleep disruption, anxiety, difficulty concentrating, and emotional numbing. Even when external life continues—work, relationships, responsibilities—the internal emotional system can remain anchored to the event that caused the injury.

In Denise Brown's public journey, what becomes significant is not the legal outcome itself, but the gradual shift in how emotional energy is directed. Over time, advocacy and structured meaning-making around prevention and awareness replaced purely internal cycles of anger. This did not erase grief, but it changed how grief functioned internally. Instead of remaining a closed loop of emotional repetition, it became outward action with purpose.

This illustrates a pattern seen across many human experiences of trauma and loss: the external world can continue to move forward while the internal world remains fixed in a specific moment. A person may function socially, professionally, and physically, yet still feel mentally confined to a past event that no longer exists in present time. This condition is not physical imprisonment, but psychological captivity—where memory becomes the structure that limits emotional freedom.

What defines this state is not the absence of life activity, but the presence of internal repetition. The mind returns to the same emotional location again and again, often under the belief that revisiting it will produce resolution. Instead, it frequently reinforces the emotional weight of the experience, keeping it active long after the external event has ended.

Chapter 5 begins here: in the lived reality of people who are no longer trapped by circumstances, but are still internally bound to them, where the prison has no physical walls, yet feels just as real.

Life Continues, But Something Has Changed

Life often continues in its expected rhythm even when the inner world has begun to carry a different condition. Responsibilities are still met, conversations still take place, and daily routines remain outwardly intact. To others, there is no visible disruption in behavior or performance. Yet within the private space of thought and feeling, something subtle has shifted. The experience of life begins to feel slightly restricted, as though an invisible weight is shaping the way each moment is internally received.

In this stage, the individual remains fully capable of functioning in social and practical environments, but the internal sense of ease begins to diminish. There is a quiet awareness that emotional freedom does not fully match external activity. The mind continues to operate, yet it does so with a reduced sense of spaciousness. Even in ordinary moments, there may be an unspoken feeling that something within is carrying more than it comfortably expresses.

As this condition develops, the contrast between outer stability and inner limitation becomes more noticeable. Life appears unchanged in structure, yet the experience of it begins to feel different in tone. This difference is not always dramatic or easily described, but it is consistently present in perception. The person begins to sense that while life is continuing forward, something within is not moving with the same sense of openness it once had.

From a psychological perspective, research on chronic emotional stress suggests that sustained internal tension can alter subjective experience of daily functioning without necessarily disrupting outward performance, creating a lived separation between external behavior and internal emotional state.[16] This helps explain how individuals may appear stable while experiencing internal restriction.

At a deeper level, this stage introduces a quiet realization. Functioning in life does not always reflect freedom within life. External continuity can coexist with internal limitation, and it is within this contrast that the awareness of emotional captivity begins to slowly emerge.

The Invisible Boundaries

As internal experience continues to develop, a subtle but important shift begins to take shape in the way memory and thought interact. Certain memories begin to carry a distinct emotional charge that influences how the mind moves through its own inner space. Without conscious decision, attention starts to organize itself around these charged areas, sometimes approaching them repeatedly, and at other times avoiding them entirely. This creates an internal pattern that feels natural, yet gradually shapes the range of emotional movement.

In this stage, though no longer flows with complete openness. Instead, it begins to follow familiar routes shaped by prior emotional intensity. Some inner themes are revisited often, especially those connected to unresolved experiences, while other areas are quietly avoided because of the discomfort they carry. This does not happen through deliberate choice, but through repeated emotional association that guides attention over time.

As these patterns continue, emotional triggers begin to produce a sense of internal contraction. A word, a memory, or even a passing thought can create a tightening within awareness that signals the presence of unresolved material. Over time, this repeated contraction influences how freely the mind explores its own inner world. What once felt open and fluid begins to feel subtly structured around emotional boundaries that were never consciously designed.

From a psychological perspective, research in cognitive and emotional processing has shown that repeated exposure to emotionally significant memories can strengthen neural pathways associated with

---

[16] Robert M. Sapolsky, *Why Zebras Don't Get Ulcers*, 3rd ed. (New York: Henry Holt and Company, 2004), 92.

those experiences, leading to preferential activation patterns and avoidance responses in related emotional contexts.[17] This helps explain how memory can begin to organize attention and perception around emotionally charged material.

At a deeper level, this stage reveals an important principle of inner life. The mind begins to construct invisible boundaries through repetition, and over time, these boundaries define the emotional territory within which thought feels most familiar and least resisted.

The Cycle of Blame

As the inner world continues to process unresolved emotional material, a repeating pattern begins to take shape in thought. The mind naturally returns to the event and begins to assign responsibility outward, forming a structured explanation that supports the internal emotional position. This process often feels automatic, as though thought itself is attempting to restore balance by identifying a clear source for the emotional disturbance.

In this stage, blame becomes a form of internal organization. The memory of what happened is revisited repeatedly, and each return strengthens the sense of justification. The emotional system experiences brief relief when clarity of responsibility is established, yet this relief does not remain stable. Soon after, the mind returns again to the same material, continuing the cycle of interpretation and re interpretation. Over time, this repetition creates a strong emotional linkage between the memory and the sense of self.

Within this cycle, conversations are often replayed internally with imagined corrections or alternative responses. The mind constructs scenarios where different outcomes could have occurred, reinforcing the emotional narrative in subtle ways. Even in moments of external distraction, the internal dialogue continues to revisit familiar emotional ground, keeping attention connected to the original event.

Gradually, emotional energy becomes increasingly tied to external figures or circumstances associated with the offense. Instead of naturally detaching over time, the emotional system continues to reference the same source as it cycles through justification and reinforcement. This creates a condition where emotional engagement remains active long after the original moment has passed.

From a psychological perspective, studies in cognitive rumination have shown that repetitive thinking patterns focused on perceived injustice or responsibility can prolong emotional activation and

---

[17] Daniel L. Schacter, *The Seven Sins of Memory: How the Mind Forgets and Remembers* (Boston: Houghton Mifflin, 2001), 118.

maintain stress related physiological responses over extended periods.[18] This helps explain how repeated internal justification can sustain emotional attachment rather than reduce it.

At a deeper level, this stage reveals a consistent principle of inner life. What is repeatedly assigned outward in thought does not simply leave the system; it continues to remain active within it, shaping emotional continuity through repetition.

Emotional Dependence on the Offense

As time continues, the memory of the offense does not remain static within the inner world. It begins to gather emotional weight through repeated attention, and what was once a single experience slowly becomes a recurring reference point in thought. The mind starts to return to this memory with increasing familiarity, and over time, the act of recollection becomes less intentional and more habitual. What was once an event beginning to function as an internal pattern of return.

In this stage, emotional experience begins to organize itself around the memory rather than around present reality. The offense is no longer simply remembered; it begins to occupy a central place in the inner narrative. Each return to the memory reinforces its emotional presence, shaping how other experiences are interpreted. Gradually, the emotional system begins to treat this memory as a stable point of reference, even in unrelated situations.

As this continues, a subtle shift occurs in identity formation. The emotional response connected to the offense begins to blend with self-perception, and the boundary between what happened and who is experiencing it becomes less distinct. Letting go begins to feel unfamiliar, not because it is impossible, but because the internal system has grown accustomed to orbiting around the same emotional center. This creates a condition where movement away from the memory feels like a departure from something structurally familiar.

From a psychological perspective, research in autobiographical memory has shown that repeated retrieval of emotionally significant events increases their accessibility and reinforces their integration into self-referential processing, making them more central to ongoing cognition and emotional regulation.[19] This helps explain how repeated

---

[18] Edward R. Watkins, "Constructive and Unconstructive Repetitive Thought," *Psychological Bulletin* 134, no. 2 (2008): 163.

[19] Dorthe Berntsen and David C. Rubin, "Emotionally Charged Autobiographical Memories Across the Life Span," *Psychology and Aging* 17, no. 4 (2002): 640.

recollection can gradually shape emotional stability around a specific memory.

At a deeper level, this stage reveals a quiet transformation. What is remembered repeatedly does not remain neutral within consciousness; it begins to influence the structure of inner stability itself, shaping the emotional world through sustained attention.

The Moment of Realization

At a certain point in the inner journey, awareness begins to turn inward with unusual clarity. The person starts to notice that emotional freedom has not remained the same as before, even though external life continues without visible interruption. There is a growing recognition that certain thought patterns return again and again, almost as if the mind is moving through familiar tracks that it cannot easily leave. This observation does not arrive as a sudden conclusion, but rather as a gradual clarity forming through repeated inner experience.

In this stage, inner dialogue begins to reveal something important. The same emotional material is revisited without significant resolution, and each return brings a similar emotional tone. The sense of movement that usually accompanies processing or healing feels reduced. Instead of progression, there is repetition. Instead of release, there is return. This creates a quiet but unmistakable awareness that something within the emotional life is holding its shape in a fixed pattern.

As this recognition deepens, the perception of emotional confinement becomes clearer. The individual begins to sense that attention is not freely moving, but repeatedly drawn back into the same internal space. This realization does not carry dramatic intensity, but it brings a sober awareness that emotional experience has become structured around what is unresolved. In this moment, the internal landscape begins to appear less like open space and more like a defined boundary system shaped by memory and emotion.

From a psychological perspective, research on repetitive negative thinking has shown that persistent cognitive loops are strongly associated with reduced emotional flexibility and increased difficulty in disengaging from emotionally charged material, contributing to a sustained sense of psychological entrapment.[20] This helps clarify how repeated thought patterns can maintain emotional captivity even in the absence of external conditions.

---

[20] Adrian Wells, "Metacognitive Therapy for Anxiety and Depression," *Cognitive and Behavioral Practice* 16, no. 4 (2009): 363.

At a deeper level, this moment marks a significant turning point. Recognition begins where captivity is finally seen, and awareness itself becomes the first step toward understanding the structure that has been shaping inner experience.

Chapter 6: The Interruption

On April 15, 2013, during the Boston Marathon in Boston, Massachusetts, two homemade bombs exploded near the finish line on Boylston Street. The attack killed three people, including an 8-year-old boy named Martin Richard, and injured more than 260 others. Among the survivors was Jeff Bauman, a spectator who had been waiting near the finish line to cheer on a friend.

Bauman was severely injured in the explosion and lost both of his legs above the knee. In the immediate aftermath, he also became a key witness, identifying one of the suspects to law enforcement while still in recovery. His life changed in an instant, not gradually or predictably, but through a sudden interruption that broke every sense of normal continuity.

In the months following the attack, Bauman underwent extensive physical rehabilitation at Spaulding Rehabilitation Hospital in Boston. Medical records and interviews documented not only the physical trauma but also the psychological impact of the event—sleep disruption, anxiety, and emotional distress typical of severe trauma exposure. His recovery required long-term medical care, prosthetic adaptation, and psychological adjustment to an entirely new physical reality.

What stands out in his public recovery journey is not only the medical progress, but the shift in meaning-making over time. In interviews and in his memoir *Stronger* (co-written with Bret Witter, published in 2014), Bauman describes how the early months after the bombing were dominated by confusion, anger, and emotional overwhelm. Life before the event and life after the event felt disconnected, as though a single moment had interrupted the entire structure of his future.

As recovery continued, something subtle changed. The interruption that initially represented only loss and destruction began to take on a different function: it forced attention into the present moment in a way that could not be avoided or ignored. Rehabilitation required daily participation, incremental progress, and repeated engagement with new physical and emotional limits. Over time, this structured engagement reduced the dominance of the initial traumatic shock response.

Psychologically, trauma research describes this phase as a disruption of automatic life patterns. When a sudden event breaks continuity, the mind loses its ability to operate on familiar assumptions. This interruption can initially intensify distress, but it also creates the first opening where new perception becomes possible. The mind is no longer running on old patterns uninterrupted; something has broken the cycle long enough for awareness to enter differently.

Bauman's story is not about the event itself being resolved quickly, nor about suffering being erased. It is about how a single interruption can force a human life out of automatic emotional repetition and into conscious reorientation. In that space, even pain becomes something that must be reprocessed rather than endlessly repeated in the same form.

This is the entry point of Chapter 6: the moment when something breaks the expected emotional pattern long enough for awareness to become visible again—not as resolution, but as interruption.

A Moment That Breaks the Pattern

The internal rhythm of resentment often develops its own consistency, shaping thought patterns that feel familiar and stable even when they are emotionally heavy. In this stage of the human experience, the mind tends to circle within established interpretations of past events, returning again and again to the same emotional conclusions. It becomes a structured inner environment where familiar memories and judgments occupy most of the reflective space. Yet within such continuity, there are rare moments when something external enters the inner world with enough weight to disturb its repetition.

At an unexpected point, the emotional system encounters a different kind of input that does not align with the established narrative. It may arrive through a conversation, a moment of teaching, or a reflective insight that carries a different moral and psychological perspective. The immediate effect is not acceptance but interruption. The mind pauses in its habitual sequence, and for a brief interval, the inner repetition loses its automatic flow. This interruption does not resolve the internal conflict, but it introduces a gap where reflection becomes possible in a new way.

During this interruption, the familiar internal justification begins to lose its uninterrupted dominance. Thoughts that once moved in a closed loop begin to encounter alternative interpretations. The emotional structure that was previously self-reinforcing now experiences a moment of instability. In this space, awareness begins to shift from pure reaction toward observation. The individual becomes aware that their internal narrative has been running in a repetitive cycle, even if no immediate change in emotion occurs.

This kind of disruption is often the first point at which forgiveness enters human awareness as more than a distant moral idea. It appears instead as a confronting possibility that challenges the permanence of emotional conclusions. Research in clinical psychology has observed that even brief cognitive interruptions in repetitive negative thought patterns can reduce the intensity of emotional fixation by creating space for reappraisal and reinterpretation of past events.[21] This indicates that change often begins not with emotional resolution, but with interruption of continuity.

Spiritual reflection adds another dimension to this experience. Moments of interruption frequently arrive before full understanding develops. They function as openings rather than conclusions, creating space for awareness to expand beyond established emotional boundaries. In such moments, the internal system of resentment is not yet transformed, but it is no longer entirely uninterrupted. A new possibility has entered the field of perception.

Exposure to the Idea of Forgiveness

Within the continuity of an established emotional narrative, the introduction of a new concept does not immediately transform perception. Instead, it enters as an unfamiliar presence that carries both intellectual clarity and emotional weight. Forgiveness, when first encountered in this stage, is not received as a simple moral suggestion, but as a concept that directly interacts with deeply held emotional conclusions. It stands in contrast to the internal structure that has been built around memory, interpretation, and perceived justice.

The initial response to this concept is often resistance that arises quietly within thought. The mind begins to compare two internal positions that appear incompatible. One position is rooted in the desire for justice, where emotional injury demands acknowledgment and balance. The other position introduces the possibility of release, where emotional holding is no longer required as a form of resolution. This comparison creates an internal tension, because both ideas appear valid at different levels of awareness, yet they cannot be fully integrated without inner adjustment.

As this new possibility remains present in awareness, emotional discomfort begins to surface. The idea of letting go does not feel neutral,

---

[21] Everett L. Worthington Jr. and Michael E. Scherer, "Forgiveness Is an Emotion Focused Coping Strategy That Can Reduce Health Risks and Improve Health Outcomes," *Journal of Clinical Psychology* 60, no. 6 (2004): 620.

because it interacts directly with memory that still carries emotional charge. The discomfort is not caused by misunderstanding, but by the collision between established emotional attachment and emerging conceptual awareness. In this phase, forgiveness is not yet an internal experience; it is an idea being examined under the pressure of existing emotional structure.

Psychologically, this stage reflects the early formation of cognitive dissonance, where belief systems and emotional attachments begin to operate in tension with one another. Research in interpersonal forgiveness has shown that exposure to forgiveness frameworks can initially increase internal conflict before any emotional resolution takes place, as individuals evaluate forgiveness in relation to perceived fairness and emotional injury.[22] This demonstrates that the introduction of forgiveness often functions first as disruption before it becomes integration.

At a deeper level of reflection, this moment represents the entry of a new possibility into the inner world. It has not yet been embraced, but it has been acknowledged. That acknowledgment alone begins to expand the boundaries of internal perception. A new direction becomes visible, even while the heart remains anchored to previous emotional conclusions.

Resistance and Inner Argument

When the idea of forgiveness remains present in awareness beyond its initial introduction, the inner system that has been formed around emotional injury begins to respond with structured resistance. This response is not random; it follows the logic of preservation, where the existing interpretation of events seeks to maintain its coherence. The mind begins to defend the established narrative of harm, not only as a memory but as a framework that has organized emotional meaning over time.

At this stage, forgiveness is often evaluated through the lens of fairness. The internal dialogue strengthens the position that what occurred carries a weight that requires acknowledgment before any form of release can be considered. This creates a mental reinforcement loop, where recollection of the original offense becomes more vivid as it is repeatedly used to support the argument for emotional holding. The memory is no longer passive; it becomes actively recruited into the defense of the present emotional state.

---

[22] Michael E. McCullough, Everett L. Worthington Jr., and Kenneth C. Rachal, "Interpersonal Forgiving in Close Relationships," *Journal of Personality and Social Psychology* 73, no. 2 (1997): 324.

As this process continues, the emotional identity begins to participate in its own defense. The individual does not only remember what happened, but begins to experience the remembering as part of who they are in relation to the event. Any suggestion of reinterpretation feels like a challenge to personal coherence, because the established narrative has become integrated into self-understanding. In this condition, resistance does not simply oppose forgiveness; it protects continuity of identity.

This phase also reveals a psychological mechanism where thought structures resist reinterpretation when emotional attachment is strong. Studies in cognitive and emotional processing of forgiveness indicate that individuals often experience heightened internal argumentation when confronted with alternative interpretations of past harm, as the mind works to preserve emotional consistency and perceived moral balance.[23] This demonstrates that resistance is often a sign of deep attachment rather than mere disagreement.

From a reflective standpoint, this inner argument becomes evidence of attachment itself. The intensity of resistance reveals the degree to which emotional memory has been integrated into internal structure. What appears as opposition to forgiveness is, at a deeper level, confirmation that the emotional experience still holds influence within the inner world.

The Tension Between Truth and Emotion

As the process of internal reflection continues, a new form of awareness begins to emerge within the mind. This awareness is intellectual in nature at first, allowing the individual to observe the situation with greater clarity than before. Patterns of interpretation become more visible, and the structure of emotional reasoning can be recognized with increasing precision. Yet this cognitive clarity does not immediately alter the emotional response that has been established over time.

At this stage, the mind and the emotional system begin to operate in parallel yet distinct layers. The intellectual aspect may acknowledge alternative interpretations, including the possibility of release or reinterpretation, while the emotional system remains anchored to the original experience of injury. This creates an internal division where understanding and feeling do not yet converge into a unified response.

---

[23] Frank D. Fincham, Julie Hall, and Steven R. Beach, "Forgiveness in Marriage: Current Status and Future Directions," *Family Relations* 55, no. 4 (2006): 415.

The presence of awareness does not automatically dissolve the intensity of emotional memory.

In moments of reflection, the individual may briefly perceive the situation from a broader perspective, recognizing patterns that were previously unseen. However, these moments are often followed by a return to established emotional responses, as the deeper emotional imprint continues to exert influence. This oscillation between insight and emotional return becomes a defining feature of this stage, revealing the gradual nature of internal transformation.

Psychologically, this reflects the coexistence of dual processing systems, where cognitive appraisal and emotional memory operate through different neural pathways. Research in emotional regulation has shown that individuals can maintain intellectual understanding of a situation while still experiencing persistent emotional activation linked to the same memory, indicating that cognition and emotion do not always change in unison.[24] This explains why awareness alone does not immediately result in emotional release.

From a reflective standpoint, this phase represents a critical developmental tension. The expansion of understanding creates space for potential change, yet the emotional system continues to preserve the original imprint. The individual stands between recognition and transformation, experiencing the distance between knowing and becoming.

The First Internal Question

As the internal process continues beyond initial interruption and resistance, a subtle but important shift begins to form within awareness. The mind, which previously held a stable and defended interpretation of the emotional past, starts to generate a quieter form of inquiry. This inquiry does not arise from external pressure, but from an internal recognition that sustained emotional holding has carried a cost that extends beyond the original event.

In this stage, reflection becomes more personal and less defensive. The individual begins to observe the effects of long-term emotional attachment on inner experience, including its influence on peace, clarity, and emotional energy. This observation does not immediately dissolve the established narrative, yet it introduces a new level of honesty within self-awareness. The emotional position that once felt fixed begins to show subtle signs of flexibility.

---

[24] Richard S. Lazarus and Susan Folkman, *Stress, Appraisal, and Coping* (New York: Springer Publishing Company, 1984), 158.

With this emerging awareness, the possibility of release begins to enter thought as a serious consideration rather than a distant or abstract idea. The internal certainty that previously supported emotional holding starts to soften, not through force, but through recognition of internal consequence. This softening does not yet equal forgiveness, but it creates the psychological space in which forgiveness can eventually be considered without immediate rejection.

Psychological research on cognitive reappraisal in emotional regulation suggests that when individuals begin to evaluate the personal cost of sustained emotional states, they become more open to alternative interpretations and coping strategies, including forgiveness-oriented responses.[25] This indicates that internal questioning often serves as a preparatory stage for deeper emotional change.

At a deeper level of reflection, this moment represents the beginning of transition. The interruption that first disturbed emotional continuity now develops into inquiry. What was once accepted without question becomes subject to reconsideration, and within that reconsideration, the pathway toward transformation begins to quietly form.

[25] James J. Gross, "Emotion Regulation: Affective, Cognitive, and Social Consequences," *Psychophysiology* 39, no. 3 (2002): 282.

Chapter 7: The Mirror Moment

On June 17, 2015, in Charleston, South Carolina, a 21-year-old white supremacist named Dylann Roof entered the historic Mother Emanuel African Methodist Episcopal Church during a Bible study session. He spent time with the congregation before opening fire, killing nine African American worshippers, including Pastor and State Senator Clementa C. Pinckney. The attack was one of the most devastating acts of racially motivated violence in modern American church history.

What followed in the days after the shooting was not only national grief but also a striking moment of public emotional response that later became widely studied. On June 19, 2015, during Roof's bond hearing in Charleston, family members of the victims were given the opportunity to speak directly to him in court. These brief statements, delivered in the courtroom, became widely broadcast and documented across the United States.

Among them was Ethel Lance's daughter, Nadine Collier, who spoke through tears directly to the accused. She said she forgave him—not as a dismissal of what happened, but as a release of the emotional burden she could no longer carry. Her words were simple, not performative, but deeply personal. She described her mother's absence and then added that she was choosing forgiveness because holding on to hatred was no longer something she could live with.

What is significant in moments like this is not that pain disappears, but that it becomes fully visible without disguise. Psychological research on grief and trauma shows that in the aftermath of sudden violent loss, individuals often experience intense emotional states including anger, sleep disturbance, intrusive thoughts, and prolonged grief reactions. These are not abstract conditions—they affect daily functioning, concentration, physical health, and emotional regulation.

In interviews following the hearing, several family members of the victims described how the public act of speaking in court forced them to look directly at their own emotional condition in a way they had not done before. The experience was not only about addressing the perpetrator, but also about recognizing what the trauma had been doing internally—how grief and anger had been living inside them alongside love, memory, and loss.

Clinical trauma studies often describe this stage as "self-confrontation," where the emotional reality of the survivor becomes as important as the event itself. It is not just about what happened externally, but about what continues to happen internally when the memory is revisited repeatedly. In such moments, people begin to notice something uncomfortable but clarifying: the most persistent effects of harm are no longer external—they are internal patterns of thought, emotion, and bodily response.

This is why Nadine Collier's words became widely remembered. Not because they changed what had happened, but because they revealed something happening inside her in real time: a recognition that holding onto anger was shaping her own emotional world as much as the memory itself. Forgiveness, in that moment, was not presented as forgetting or excusing, but as an honest acknowledgment of internal reality.

The "mirror moment" is this stage of human experience where attention turns away from the other person long enough to see the self clearly. Not the self as defined by what was done, but the self as shaped by what is being carried. It is often uncomfortable because it removes emotional distance. There is no longer only "what they did," but also "what it is doing to me."

Chapter 7 begins here: at the point where the human being can no longer look outward alone, because the truth has begun to reflect inward as well.

The Moment of Self Confrontation

There are moments in inner life when attention shifts in a way that feels subtle at first, yet alters the direction of awareness. The mind, which has long been oriented toward external causes and interpretations, begins to turn inward with a different quality of observation. In this stage, emotional experience is no longer viewed primarily through the actions of others, but through the condition it has created within the self.

As this inward attention strengthens, defensive explanations that once supported emotional stability begin to lose some of their influence. The narrative that focused on what was done, what was said, and what should have been different starts to recede in intensity. In its place, a quieter form of recognition emerges, one that does not depend on external validation or argument. This recognition does not arrive with force, but with clarity that gradually becomes unavoidable.

With this shift in focus, the individual begins to observe internal emotional conditions more directly. The experience of bitterness, previously interpreted through external events, is now seen as part of internal reality. This change in perception creates a new kind of honesty, where attention is directed toward what is being carried within rather than what has been received from outside. The emotional state begins to appear less like a response and more like an ongoing internal environment.

Psychological research on self-focused attention suggests that when individuals shift from external attribution toward internal observation, emotional processing becomes more reflective and less reactive, allowing previously unexamined emotional patterns to enter conscious awareness.[26] This transition marks an important step in emotional recognition, where perception begins to separate from justification.

From a reflective standpoint, this moment represents the beginning of clarity without escape. What is seen internally is no longer filtered primarily through explanation or defense. Instead, awareness begins to rest on direct observation. In this quiet shift, the foundation is laid for deeper understanding of internal emotional life.

Seeing Bitterness Without Justification

As inward attention deepens beyond initial self-confrontation, perception begins to shift from explanation toward observation. In this stage, emotional experience is no longer filtered through immediate reasoning or external comparison. Instead, it becomes something that can be seen directly within awareness. Bitterness, which was previously embedded within justification and memory, begins to appear as an internal presence that can be recognized without the need for defense.

This recognition introduces a new kind of emotional clarity. The individual begins to observe internal states with less dependence on interpretive narratives. What once required explanation now becomes visible in its own form. Bitterness is no longer experienced only as a response to external events, but as an ongoing internal condition that exists within the present moment of awareness. This shift does not immediately remove emotional intensity, but it changes the way that intensity is understood.

As this clarity strengthens, justifications that once supported emotional holding begin to lose their structural influence. The mind's

---

[26] Thomas D. Borkovec, "The Nature, Functions, and Origins of Worry," in *Worrying: Perspectives on Theory, Assessment and Treatment*, ed. Graham C. L. Davey and Adrian Wells (Chichester: Wiley, 2006), 112.

effort to maintain a consistent narrative around past events becomes less compelling when compared to direct observation of present internal state. Emotional honesty begins to take precedence over emotional argument, allowing awareness to rest more on what is experienced rather than what is defended.

In psychological terms, this reflects the emergence of meta-awareness, where the individual becomes aware of their own cognitive and emotional processes as objects of observation rather than automatic reactions. Research in cognitive psychology has shown that this form of awareness can reduce the dominance of habitual emotional responses by introducing a reflective distance between stimulus and interpretation.[27] This shift allows previously automatic defense patterns to weaken under sustained observation.

From a deeper reflective perspective, this moment represents a quiet transformation in perception. What was once fully justified begins to be seen as internal condition. This does not immediately resolve emotional content, but it changes its meaning within awareness, opening space for further internal reorganization.

The Recognition of Internal Cost

As awareness continues to deepen, attention begins to shift from the origin of pain toward its present effect within the inner life. What once appeared as a justified emotional position gradually reveals its ongoing influence on personal experience. The focus moves from external causes toward internal consequences, where the sustained holding of bitterness is now seen in terms of what it produces within the self rather than what initiated it.

At this stage, the effects of prolonged emotional attachment begin to register with greater clarity. There is a growing awareness of mental fatigue, emotional heaviness, and a reduction in inner vitality that accompanies continuous remembrance of injury. The individual begins to observe that the mind carries a kind of weight that is not related to present circumstances alone, but to the persistence of unresolved emotional content. This recognition introduces a new form of honesty, where internal experience is evaluated in its current state rather than its historical justification.

Reflection becomes increasingly self-directed. Instead of returning repeatedly to external blame, attention begins to rest on the internal condition that has developed over time. Emotional holding is no longer

---

[27] Jonathan D. Teasdale et al., "Metacognitive Awareness and Prevention of Relapse in Depression: Empirical Evidence," *Journal of Consulting and Clinical Psychology* 70, no. 2 (2002): 279.

viewed only as a response to past events, but as an ongoing internal expenditure that shapes present awareness. In this way, the cost of attachment becomes more difficult to ignore, as it is experienced directly within thought, energy, and emotional stability.

This unfolding awareness resonates with the biblical reflection that prolonged inner burden affects the whole person, as expressed in the words, "Heaviness in the heart of man maketh it stoop" (Proverbs 12:25). At the same time, a contrasting spiritual invitation appears in the teaching, "Come unto me, all ye that labour and are heavy laden, and I will give you rest" (Matthew 11:28). These verses together illuminate the tension between carrying internal weight and the possibility of release, where emotional experience and spiritual invitation intersect within human awareness.

From a psychological perspective, research on self-focused appraisal indicates that when individuals begin to evaluate the personal impact of sustained emotional states, attention shifts away from external attribution and toward internal experience, increasing awareness of how thought patterns influence emotional and physical well-being.[28] This shift allows the cost of emotional holding to become directly observable within lived experience.

At a deeper level, this stage marks a quiet but significant realization. What is held internally does not remain static; it shapes the quality of inner life over time. This awareness does not yet resolve the emotional content, but it establishes clarity about its ongoing influence within the self.

The Mirror Moment of Truth

As internal awareness reaches greater stability, perception begins to settle into a more direct form of recognition. The emotional landscape that was once interpreted through external causes is now seen with reduced distortion. Bitterness is no longer primarily understood as something produced by events alone, but as an internal condition that has developed sustained presence within consciousness. This shift marks a transition from explanation to observation.

In this moment of clarity, the individual begins to recognize that emotional states are not only received but also maintained through continued inner agreement. The persistence of resentment is no longer viewed solely as the consequence of past actions, but also as something that has been carried forward through ongoing internal attention. This realization introduces a quiet form of responsibility, not as

---

[28] James J. Gross, "Emotion Regulation: Current Status and Future Prospects," *Psychological Inquiry* 26, no. 1 (2015): 7.

condemnation, but as awareness of participation in sustaining emotional experience.

The awareness that emerges here is often accompanied by a deep sense of stillness. Instead of defending or analyzing the emotional state, the mind begins to observe it directly. Bitterness is seen as it is, without the layers of justification that previously surrounded it. This form of recognition does not immediately resolve emotional content, but it allows the truth of the internal condition to become visible without resistance.

This clarity resonates with the biblical reflection, "The light of the body is the eye: if therefore thine eye be single, thy whole body shall be full of light" (Matthew 6:22). In this context, single vision represents undivided awareness, where perception is no longer split between justification and truth. Another layer of reflection appears in the words, "Create in me a clean heart, O God; and renew a right spirit within me" (Psalm 51:10), which speaks to the transformation that begins when internal truth is acknowledged without resistance.

Psychologically, this stage reflects the integration of self-awareness with emotional acknowledgment, where cognitive and emotional systems begin to align around a shared recognition of present internal state.[29] Research in self-regulation suggests that such integration often marks a turning point in emotional processing, as individuals move from interpretive defense toward experiential acceptance.

From a deeper spiritual perspective, truth becomes transformative when it is fully seen without resistance. In this moment, recognition replaces justification as the dominant inner experience, allowing awareness to rest in what is real rather than what is defended.

---

[29] Daniel M. Wegner, "Ironic Processes of Mental Control," *Psychological Review* 101, no. 1 (1994): 38.

Chapter 8: The War Within

On January 8, 2011, in Tucson, Arizona, a public event outside a supermarket became one of the most widely reported shootings in modern U.S. history. A gunman, **Jared Lee Loughner**, opened fire during a constituent meeting held by U.S. Representative **Gabrielle Giffords**. Six people were killed, and Giffords herself was critically injured, suffering a gunshot wound to the head that left her with severe brain trauma.

In the immediate aftermath, Giffords was rushed to Banner University Medical Center in Tucson, where she underwent emergency brain surgery performed by neurosurgeon Dr. Michael Lemole. Her survival was uncertain in the first hours. Medical records and later rehabilitation reports documented the severity of her injuries, including aphasia (difficulty with language), physical impairment, and a long and demanding recovery process that required months of speech therapy, physical rehabilitation, and cognitive retraining.

What made her case widely studied was not only survival, but the internal psychological struggle that followed. In interviews published after her recovery progressed, Giffords and her husband, astronaut Mark Kelly, described the emotional complexity of recovery—not only physical healing, but the ongoing internal processing of trauma, fear, and memory. Although she did not publicly engage in language of personal forgiveness toward the shooter in the way some other trauma narratives do, her life reflects a deeper reality documented in trauma psychology: recovery often involves a prolonged internal conflict between anger, fear, meaning reconstruction, and the effort to rebuild identity after violent disruption.

In the years following the shooting, Giffords founded the organization Giffords: Courage to Fight Gun Violence, established in 2013. Her public work shifted toward advocacy and prevention, transforming personal trauma into structured social action. Interviews with rehabilitation specialists who worked with her describe how recovery was not a single emotional shift, but a long negotiation between what had happened, what was remembered, and what life would now become.

Clinically, trauma experts often describe this stage as an "internal conflict state," where the mind simultaneously tries to protect itself from harm while also attempting to integrate the reality of what has already occurred. One part of the psyche seeks safety through avoidance, suppression, or anger. Another part seeks meaning, adaptation, and forward movement. These two internal systems can operate at the same time, producing what feels like emotional contradiction within the same person.

This is the "war within" that defines this chapter. It is not a battle between people, but a tension inside one mind. The memory of injury does not disappear, but neither does the need to continue living. Fear competes with hope. Anger competes with understanding. Self-protection competes with emotional release. And neither side fully resolves immediately.

Gabrielle Giffords' recovery illustrates this internal duality in a very human way. Healing did not arrive as emotional simplicity. It arrived as layered reconstruction—physical, cognitive, and emotional—where different parts of experience did not always move at the same speed. The body learned again how to function. The mind learned again how to process language. And the emotional world slowly learned how to live with memory without being entirely controlled by it.

Chapter 8 begins here: at the point where the human being is no longer dealing with a single wound, but with competing internal forces that define how that wound will be carried forward.

The Emergence of Internal Conflict

As awareness continues to develop beyond recognition and reflection, the inner life begins to experience a deeper form of tension. The idea of forgiveness, once seen as distant or conceptual, now enters the emotional field in a way that creates internal movement rather than simple observation. This movement does not immediately resolve anything; instead, it introduces competing impulses within the mind that begin to operate at the same time.

One part of the inner world leans toward justice, holding firmly to the sense that emotional truth requires acknowledgment and balance. Another part begins to sense the possibility of mercy, a quieter invitation toward release and softness of heart. These two movements do not easily coexist without tension, because each carries its own sense of moral and emotional validity. The result is an internal experience where awareness itself becomes charged with conflict.

In this stage, the individual becomes more conscious of the emotional weight attached to both holding and releasing. Justice feels connected to dignity, truth, and personal integrity, while mercy introduces the idea of loosening emotional grip. The mind begins to feel pressure between these directions, as if standing between two forms of internal loyalty. This creates a state where awareness is active, yet unresolved, and thought becomes increasingly reflective.

This inner division is reflected in the biblical tension between justice and mercy, where Scripture speaks of both accountability and compassion, saying, "Mercy and truth are met together; righteousness and peace have kissed each other" (Psalm 85:10). At the same time, the call toward release appears in the words, "Be ye kind one to another, tenderhearted, forgiving one another, even as God for Christ's sake hath forgiven you" (Ephesians 4:32). These passages together reveal that the struggle within the human heart is often a space where opposing spiritual realities are held in tension before understanding matures.

Psychologically, this stage reflects the activation of competing cognitive and emotional value systems, where moral reasoning and emotional attachment begin to operate simultaneously without immediate integration.[30] This creates internal pressure that signals the presence of unresolved emotional material now entering conscious awareness.

From a deeper perspective, this condition of inner division often precedes transformation. Awareness without resolution creates pressure within the system of thought and feeling, and it is within this pressure that the possibility of change begins to quietly form.

Justice as Emotional Identity

As the internal conflict continues to develop, the sense of justice begins to take on a deeper and more personal form. It is no longer experienced only as a moral principle or an abstract idea of fairness, but gradually becomes intertwined with personal dignity and self-understanding. The emotional memory of what was endured starts to feel inseparable from the sense of who the person is, shaping how truth itself is internally defined.

In this stage, holding on to emotional pain begins to feel justified within the inner moral structure. The mind creates a strong connection between remembering the offense and preserving personal worth. Letting go of the pain can begin to feel, within this internal framework, as if it risks diminishing the seriousness of what was experienced. As a result, emotional retention is quietly supported by a sense of protecting truth.

---

[30] Tania Singer and Klaus R. Scherer, "The Neurophysiology of Emotion: The Role of Cognitive and Affective Processes," *Trends in Cognitive Sciences* 19, no. 6 (2015): 325.

The past injury is no longer only a remembered event; it becomes part of how self-respect is interpreted. The inner narrative begins to protect the memory as though it carries moral responsibility. This creates a condition where emotional attachment is no longer maintained only by feeling, but also by meaning. The heart begins to defend its position as something necessary for preserving identity.

This condition reflects the deeper human tendency described in Scripture, where the heart becomes closely linked with inner direction and meaning, as it is written, "Keep thy heart with all diligence; for out of it are the issues of life" (Proverbs 4:23). At the same time, the tension of holding moral injury is softened by the reminder, "Dearly beloved, avenge not yourselves, but rather give place unto wrath: for it is written, Vengeance is mine; I will repay, saith the Lord" (Romans 12:19). These words introduce a different understanding of justice that does not depend on emotional preservation.

Psychologically, moral cognition begins reinforcing emotional persistence, where belief systems and identity structures support the continuation of emotional attachment rather than its release.[31] Over time, justice is no longer held as a principle alone, but begins to function as part of identity itself.

At this point, justice becomes identity rather than principle, and what was once a moral response to pain now becomes a defining structure of self-perception.

The Fear of Letting Go

As the inner struggle deepens, another force begins to shape the emotional landscape, and that is fear. This fear does not always appear as something obvious or dramatic, but often emerges quietly within thought patterns that surround the idea of release. Letting go begins to feel like stepping into uncertainty, where the familiar structure of emotional memory no longer provides the same sense of internal control or orientation.

Within this experience, vulnerability becomes closely associated with the act of release. The mind begins to interpret emotional holding as a form of protection, as though maintaining the memory of pain preserves a necessary boundary. There is a concern that if the emotional grip is loosened, the clarity of personal truth may become blurred, and the significance of what was endured might lose its internal weight. In this way, emotional retention is linked with self-preservation.

---

[31] Jonathan Haidt, *The Righteous Mind: Why Good People Are Divided by Politics and Religion* (New York: Pantheon Books, 2012), 123.

The fear also extends toward the possibility of repetition. There is an internal anticipation that similar harm could occur again if emotional defenses are softened. This creates a sense that holding on to pain provides a form of safety, even if it carries internal cost. Emotional safety, in this stage, becomes closely associated with memory itself, and release begins to feel like exposure rather than freedom.

Scripture gently speaks into this condition, where fear and trust are placed in contrast, saying, "There is no fear in love; but perfect love casteth out fear" (1 John 4:18). At the same time, the invitation toward trust is expressed in the words, "Trust in the Lord with all thine heart; and lean not unto thine own understanding" (Proverbs 3:5). These verses introduce a different foundation for safety, one that is not dependent on emotional retention.

Psychologically, threat perception activates internal systems of emotional preservation, where the mind prioritizes continuity of protection over emotional release.[32] This response strengthens attachment to familiar emotional structures, even when those structures carry ongoing distress.

Within this dynamic, fear sustains emotional attachment more than memory itself, because it continually reinforces the sense that letting go carries greater risk than holding on.

Misunderstanding Forgiveness

As the inner conflict continues to mature, one of the strongest barriers to emotional movement arises not from the pain itself, but from the way forgiveness is understood within the mind. At this stage, forgiveness is often interpreted through distorted meanings that shape emotional resistance. It is commonly mistaken as approval of wrongdoing, as though releasing bitterness would somehow validate the injustice that was experienced.

This misunderstanding creates a strong internal tension, because the heart attempts to preserve both moral integrity and emotional relief at the same time. Forgiveness is also confused with forgetting, leading to the belief that release would erase memory or diminish truth. In reality, memory and forgiveness operate in different dimensions of inner experience, yet in this stage they are often merged in thought, producing hesitation toward any form of letting go.

There is also a belief that forgiveness removes accountability, as though emotional release would cancel the seriousness of what occurred. This interpretation strengthens resistance, because the mind

---

[32] Joseph E. LeDoux, *The Emotional Brain: The Mysterious Underpinnings of Emotional Life* (New York: Simon & Schuster, 1996), 211.

feels responsible for preserving justice through emotional holding. As a result, forgiveness is viewed not as healing, but as a form of surrendering truth. This creates a conceptual blockage that keeps emotional patterns active.

Scripture brings clarity into this confusion, where forgiveness is presented not as denial of truth, but as release from emotional captivity, saying, "Be kind to one another, tenderhearted, forgiving one another, as God in Christ forgave you" (Ephesians 4:32). At the same time, accountability remains within divine order, as expressed in, "For we must all appear before the judgment seat of Christ" (2 Corinthians 5:10). These verses together show that release and accountability are not opposites, but distinct realities.

Psychologically, conceptual distortion delays emotional processing, because the mind cannot release what it has not correctly defined.[33] When meaning is unclear, emotional systems remain in protective mode, maintaining resistance as a form of internal stability.

From a deeper perspective, truth requires correction of misunderstanding before acceptance becomes possible. As clarity slowly enters awareness, resistance begins to lose structure, and emotional rigidity starts to soften.

The Turning Pressure Point

As the internal struggle continues without resolution, the emotional system begins to experience a different kind of exhaustion. The conflict between justice and resistance, once fueled by strong emotional energy, starts to lose its intensity simply through persistence. What once felt like moral certainty and protective strength begins to feel increasingly heavy to maintain within the inner world.

At this stage, neither holding on nor resisting inward change provides genuine relief. The mind continues to return to familiar arguments, yet these arguments no longer bring the same sense of satisfaction or stability. Emotional patterns that once felt necessary begin to feel repetitive, as though the inner system is circling the same ground without movement. This creates a growing sense of saturation, where emotional space feels occupied but no longer productive.

Within this saturation, awareness begins to shift. The individual becomes more conscious of the cost of continued internal conflict. There is a quiet recognition that something within is asking for resolution, not through further justification, but through a different form

---

[33] Everett L. Worthington Jr., *Forgiveness and Reconciliation: Theory and Application* (New York: Routledge, 2006), 58.

of response. The emotional system, through exhaustion rather than persuasion, begins to loosen its resistance.

Scripture gently reflects this movement toward inner release, saying, “Come unto me, all ye that labour and are heavy laden, and I will give you rest” (Matthew 11:28). In the same spirit, another word brings direction to the burdened heart, “Cast thy burden upon the Lord, and he shall sustain thee” (Psalm 55:22). These passages speak into the moment where carrying emotional weight becomes unsustainable within the human experience.

Psychologically, sustained conflict fatigue reduces resistance strength, as the nervous system gradually shifts away from heightened defensive activation toward energy conservation.[34] This reduction in internal arousal creates space for new emotional responses to emerge.

At this point, sustained tension begins to create readiness for change, not through sudden decision, but through the natural weakening of internal opposition.

---

[34] Bruce S. McEwen, “Protective and Damaging Effects of Stress Mediators,” *New England Journal of Medicine* 338, no. 3 (1998): 172.

Chapter 9: Forgiveness and Its Boundaries

On October 2, 2006, in Nickel Mines, Pennsylvania, a small Amish schoolhouse was entered by a gunman named **Charles Carl Roberts IV**. He took several schoolgirls hostage before killing five young girls and injuring others, then taking his own life at the scene. The event shocked the United States not only because of its brutality, but because of the unexpected response that followed from the Amish community.

Within hours of the tragedy, members of the Amish community began visiting the family of the gunman. They offered condolences and even forgiveness publicly. **Amish elders and neighbors attended Roberts' funeral**, a decision that surprised much of the outside world. The response was widely reported in national media, including coverage by *The New York Times* and *CNN* in October 2006, highlighting the Amish emphasis on forgiveness and non-retaliation.

However, what is often overlooked in simplified retellings is that forgiveness in this context did not mean unrestricted access, emotional merging, or absence of boundaries. In the years following the event, Amish families did not reopen their lives to the circumstances that had caused harm. They rebuilt the school elsewhere. They maintained separation from the causes of harm. Their forgiveness existed alongside clear structural boundaries designed to protect life, children, and community stability.

Psychological observers who studied the Amish response noted something important: their act of forgiveness was not equivalent to denial of harm or removal of consequences. It was a separation between internal emotional release and external protective structure. The community did not carry long-term cycles of revenge, which often contribute to chronic stress responses in individuals and groups exposed to trauma. At the same time, they did not eliminate the need for safety, distance, and reconstruction of physical and social boundaries.

This distinction is critical in understanding human emotional health. Clinical studies on trauma and grief show that unresolved anger and prolonged rumination can contribute to long-term physiological stress effects—such as sleep disturbance, anxiety, and elevated stress hormone activity. However, these studies also emphasize that emotional release does not require exposure to ongoing harm. In other words, a person can release internal resentment while still maintaining external distance from harmful conditions.

In the Amish community's response, both realities were present. There was a release of vengeance-driven emotional cycles, but there was also a clear decision not to restore previous conditions that had enabled harm. Forgiveness was not confusion; it was clarity about what belongs inside the heart and what must remain outside of it.

This is where the deeper tension of Chapter 9 emerges. Many people assume forgiveness means restoring everything to its original state, but human experience shows otherwise. Emotional release and relational boundaries can exist at the same time. One does not cancel the other. In fact, when they are confused, people often either remain trapped in bitterness or expose themselves repeatedly to harm under the assumption that forgiveness requires unlimited access.

The Nickel Mines response became widely studied in psychology, sociology, and religious ethics because it demonstrated a rare balance: profound emotional release without collapse of protective structure. The community grieved deeply, supported the affected families, and at the same time rebuilt physical and social space to ensure safety for the future.

Chapter 9 begins here: at the point where forgiveness is no longer confused with exposure, and where emotional release is understood as something that can coexist with wise, protective boundaries.

The Need for Clarity After Conflict

After the long passage through emotional struggle and internal tension, the mind reaches a stage where confusion itself becomes one of the final barriers to peace. The emotional system has already experienced resistance, reflection, and pressure, yet without a clear understanding of forgiveness, the inner world continues to remain unsettled. It is often not the absence of willingness that prevents release, but the absence of clarity regarding what release truly means.

In this stage, forgiveness is often held within unclear definitions that sustain emotional hesitation. When the mind cannot accurately define what it is being asked to do, the emotional system remains in a protective mode. It continues to preserve old interpretations because uncertainty feels unsafe. As a result, emotional attachment persists not only through memory, but through conceptual confusion.

The necessity of clarity becomes evident when the mind begins to recognize that emotional systems cannot release what is still misidentified. When forgiveness is wrongly associated with denial or loss of truth, the heart naturally resists it as a threat to integrity. Yet when understanding begins to shift, space opens within awareness for a more stable interpretation to emerge. In this way, clarity does not force change, but prepares the inner world for it.

Scripture speaks into this moment of inner preparation, saying, "If any of you lack wisdom, let him ask of God, that giveth to all men liberally" (James 1:5). In another place, light is associated with understanding and stability, as it is written, "The entrance of thy words giveth light; it giveth understanding unto the simple" (Psalm 119:130). These words reflect the principle that clarity brings structure to the inner life, allowing confusion to dissolve.

Psychologically, ambiguity sustains emotional attachment by preventing closure of meaning systems, keeping unresolved experiences active within cognitive-emotional loops.[35] When meaning remains undefined, emotional release cannot stabilize, because the system continues searching for resolution within the same framework.

From this point of view, confusion preserves captivity, while clarity begins the process of release. It is here that the mind becomes ready not only to understand forgiveness, but to eventually experience it as a coherent internal reality.

Forgiveness Is Not Denial of Truth

As understanding deepens beyond initial confusion, one of the most important clarifications emerges: forgiveness does not involve denial of reality. What occurred in the past remains fully acknowledged within memory. Truth is not erased, minimized, or reinterpreted in a way that distorts what actually happened. Instead, truth stands intact while the internal emotional relationship to it begins to shift.

In this stage, memory and truth continue to exist with full clarity. The mind does not lose access to what was experienced, nor does it rewrite the factual foundation of events. What begins to change is not the record of reality, but the emotional response attached to it. This separation allows the individual to hold truth without being internally controlled by it.

As this distinction becomes clearer, the inner world begins to understand that emotional release does not require factual denial. It becomes possible to remember without reliving, and to acknowledge without remaining bound. Integrity is preserved because truth is not compromised, while inner freedom begins to form through a new relationship with memory.

Scripture reflects this balance between truth and inner transformation, where truth remains central while the heart is renewed,

---

[35] Daniel Kahneman, *Thinking, Fast and Slow* (New York: Farrar, Straus and Giroux, 2011), 45.

as it is written, "And ye shall know the truth, and the truth shall make you free" (John 8:32). In another place, the presence of truth is linked with inward renewal, "Create in me a clean heart, O God; and renew a right spirit within me" (Psalm 51:10). These verses together show that freedom does not come from altering truth, but from being changed within its presence.

Psychologically, cognitive separation of memory from emotional reactivity allows the mind to retain factual recall while reducing affective charge.[36] This creates a state in which experiences remain accessible without continuously triggering emotional distress.

From this perspective, truth is preserved while emotional charge is reduced, allowing clarity and stability to coexist within the inner life.

Forgiveness Is Not Weakness

As the understanding of forgiveness continues to mature, another misconception begins to dissolve, the belief that emotional release is a sign of weakness. Within many inner narratives, letting go is initially interpreted as a loss of strength, as though releasing emotional attachment reduces personal power or diminishes moral stance. However, as reflection deepens, this interpretation begins to shift.

In reality, emotional release requires a level of internal strength that is often overlooked. It is not the absence of control, but the presence of higher regulation. The mind begins to recognize that holding onto emotional pain can become automatic, while letting go requires conscious participation. This awareness reframes forgiveness as an active internal decision rather than a passive emotional collapse.

As this process continues, strength becomes redefined. It is no longer measured by how firmly emotional memory is retained, but by the ability to govern internal responses with clarity. The shift from reaction to intentional release marks a transformation in identity itself. What once responded automatically to emotional triggers begins to develop the capacity for deliberate inner direction.

Scripture reflects this deeper understanding of strength, saying, "He that is slow to anger is better than the mighty; and he that ruleth his spirit than he that taketh a city" (Proverbs 16:32). In another place, strength is connected with inner renewal and stability, "But they that wait upon the Lord shall renew their strength; they shall mount up with wings as eagles" (Isaiah 40:31). These verses reveal that true strength is not expressed through emotional retention, but through governed spirit and renewed inner life.

---

[36] Antonio R. Damasio, *Descartes' Error: Emotion, Reason, and the Human Brain* (New York: Putnam, 1994), 140.

Psychologically, executive control processes in the brain enable regulation of automatic emotional responses, allowing intentional override of habitual affective patterns.[37] This capacity distinguishes reactive emotional behavior from conscious self-regulation.

From this perspective, release is not fragility, but mastery. It reflects the presence of internal governance, where emotional life is no longer ruled by automatic repetition but guided by deliberate awareness.

Forgiveness as Release of Emotional Debt

As clarity reaches its most stable form in this chapter, forgiveness begins to take on a precise and functional meaning within the inner life. It is understood as the release of emotional debt, where the internal sense of owed repayment is consciously set down. The mind no longer maintains a continuous record of emotional obligation tied to past events, and the heart begins to loosen its attachment to what was previously held as unresolved.

In this understanding, forgiveness does not depend upon external reconciliation or the alteration of past events. Instead, it operates within the internal structure of emotional memory. The mental system that repeatedly revisits the sense of being wronged begins to disengage from its cycle of emotional repayment. What once functioned as a repeated internal demand for balance gradually loses its influence over present awareness.

As this shift occurs, inner space becomes available for restoration. Emotional energy that was previously tied to repetition begins to return to a more neutral state of awareness. This allows the mind to experience a sense of quiet reorganization, where thought and feeling are no longer bound to unresolved cycles. The internal environment becomes more open, less constrained by emotional recurrence.

Scripture reflects this principle of release and restoration, saying, "Be kind to one another, tenderhearted, forgiving one another, even as God for Christ's sake hath forgiven you" (Ephesians 4:32). In another place, release is connected with renewal of inner life, "Casting all your care upon him; for he careth for you" (1 Peter 5:7). These verses reveal that forgiveness is not transactional adjustment, but internal transfer from burden to peace.

Psychologically, this reflects the decoupling of reward and punishment emotional loops, where the brain disengages from repetitive

---

[37] Walter Mischel et al., "Cognitive and Attentional Mechanisms in Delay of Gratification," *Journal of Personality and Social Psychology* 33, no. 2 (1976): 158.

cycles of perceived emotional debt and retaliation.[38] This allows cognitive and emotional systems to return to equilibrium.

From this perspective, forgiveness becomes understood as internal liberation rather than external agreement, where emotional freedom is restored through release rather than resolution of external conditions.

---

[38] Robert J. Ferguson, "The Psychology of Forgiveness and Its Role in Emotional Regulation," *Journal of Behavioral Medicine* 38, no. 4 (2015): 612.

Chapter 10: The Decision

On April 12, 1981, in Arlington, Virginia, **Ronald Reagan** was shot outside the Washington Hilton Hotel by John Hinckley Jr. The bullet entered near his left lung and narrowly missed his heart. He was rushed to George Washington University Hospital, where surgeons performed emergency surgery that lasted several hours. His survival was uncertain in the early stages, and his recovery required weeks of intensive medical care.

What became historically significant was not only his physical recovery, but what followed afterward in his personal reflections. In interviews and later memoir accounts, Reagan described a conscious internal process regarding how he viewed the man who tried to kill him. Over time, he made a deliberate decision not to live in sustained anger toward Hinckley. This was not described as a spontaneous emotional change, but as a settled choice in how he would carry the event forward in his mind.

In his 1990 diary entries published later in *The Reagan Diaries*, he wrote about the importance of not allowing bitterness to dominate his thinking. He did not describe forgetting what happened. He did not describe emotional denial. Instead, he described a conscious direction of thought—refusing to allow the event to control his internal life beyond its factual place in history.

Medical records and historical accounts of his recovery also note that Reagan returned to a high level of functioning after surgery, resuming his presidential duties within months. While his physical healing was remarkable for a man in his seventies, what stands out in psychological observation is how he publicly framed the event: not as something to relive internally with emotional repetition, but as something that had already occurred and would not be allowed to define his ongoing mental state.

This distinction is important. Many people assume that emotional healing must precede forgiveness. But human experience often shows the opposite pattern: a decision is made first, and emotional alignment follows gradually. In Reagan's case, the choice to not dwell in resentment was not dependent on feeling ready. It was an act of will, expressed consistently over time in how he spoke and thought about the event.

Trauma psychology supports this pattern in a broader sense. Emotional recovery is not always initiated by emotional readiness. In many cases, it begins when a person makes a stable internal decision about how they will relate to their memory going forward. That decision becomes the structure through which emotions are gradually reorganized.

What makes this moment significant is that it separates reaction from intention. Without intention, the mind naturally returns to pain in repetitive cycles. With intention, those cycles begin to weaken over time, not because the memory disappears, but because it is no longer reinforced in the same way.

Chapter 10 begins here: at the point where forgiveness is no longer something that happens to a person emotionally, but something a person chooses deliberately, even while emotions are still unsettled.

The Moment of Decision Emerges

As the inner journey continues through awareness, resistance, clarification, and reflection, a subtle but decisive shift begins to form within consciousness. Understanding alone no longer carries the same weight it once did. The mind has reached a point where insight is present, yet remaining unchanged internally begins to feel increasingly untenable. In this quiet space, awareness begins to press toward action.

At this stage, emotional systems may still carry traces of resistance, but they no longer dominate the field of awareness in the same way. There is a moment of internal stillness where reaction pauses and observation becomes clearer than impulse. Within this pause, the individual begins to recognize that continued reflection without decision no longer moves the inner life forward. Something within begins to ask for response rather than further analysis.

This moment is not driven by emotional readiness, but by the recognition that clarity itself creates responsibility. The mind becomes aware that insight carries an obligation toward direction. What has been understood intellectually begins to demand expression through choice. In this way, awareness matures into responsibility, where knowing and doing begin to converge within the will.

Scripture reflects this transition from understanding to action, saying, "But be ye doers of the word, and not hearers only, deceiving your own selves" (James 1:22). In another place, the connection between choice and life direction is emphasized, "I have set before you life and death, blessing and cursing: therefore, choose life" (Deuteronomy 30:19). These passages reveal that transformation is completed through decision, not observation alone.

Psychologically, cognitive clarity reaches a threshold where behavioral decision becomes necessary, as sustained awareness without action creates internal tension that demands resolution through choice.[39] This marks the point where perception begins to reorganize toward intentional behavior.

From this perspective, light without action remains incomplete transformation, and awareness begins its true fulfillment only when it becomes expressed through deliberate decision.

Choosing Against Emotional Resistance

As the process of decision deepens, an important inner reality becomes increasingly visible: emotional resistance does not disappear at the moment of choice. Even when clarity is present and intention is formed, the emotional system may continue to produce hesitation, discomfort, or internal reluctance. In this stage, forgiveness is not chosen because emotion has aligned, but precisely because it has not yet aligned.

Within this experience, the will begins to operate with a distinct form of independence from emotional fluctuation. The individual recognizes that action does not need to wait for emotional agreement in order to be valid. Instead, decision becomes grounded in conviction, where what is understood as right and necessary begins to guide behavior more than what is currently felt. This marks a significant shift in internal governance.

As this dynamic develops, emotional alignment is no longer treated as a prerequisite for movement. The inner life begins to understand that waiting for complete emotional comfort often delays transformation. Instead, decision becomes anchored in a deeper sense of direction, where the will chooses stability over variability. In this way, action begins to separate itself from the immediate state of feeling.

Scripture reflects this principle of choosing beyond internal resistance, saying, "For it is God which worketh in you both to will and to do of his good pleasure" (Philippians 2:13). In another place, strength of action beyond emotional fluctuation is affirmed, "I can do all things through Christ which strengtheneth me" (Philippians 4:13). These verses present the idea that action is sustained by conviction rather than emotional consistency.

Psychologically, executive function overrides affective state dependency, allowing intentional behavior to proceed even when

---

[39] Albert Bandura, *Self-Efficacy: The Exercise of Control* (New York: W. H. Freeman, 1997), 154.

emotional systems remain unstable or resistant.[40] This capacity enables decision making to remain stable despite internal emotional variation.

From this perspective, action becomes independent of emotional readiness, and transformation begins to stabilize through will rather than feeling.

Forgiveness as Intentional Act

As the understanding of forgiveness matures beyond emotional struggle and resistance, it begins to take on a more structured and deliberate form within the mind. At this stage, forgiveness is no longer perceived as something that simply happens when emotions settle, but as a conscious act of intention. The individual begins to recognize that change does not wait for emotional readiness but is initiated through deliberate internal direction.

In this shift, forgiveness is no longer limited to emotional release alone. Instead, it becomes an act of responsibility, where the mind acknowledges its role in initiating transformation. The focus moves away from waiting for feelings to align, and toward choosing a new internal posture despite emotional instability. This redefinition places agency within the will rather than within fluctuating emotional states.

As this awareness deepens, decision is understood as a form of internal governance. Rather than being governed by reaction, the inner life begins to organize itself around intentional choice. Emotional healing is no longer seen as a prerequisite for forgiveness, but as something that begins after the decision has been made. In this way, choice becomes the starting point of internal restructuring.

Scripture reflects this movement from feeling to decision, saying, "Choose you this day whom ye will serve" (Joshua 24:15). In another place, the priority of inward commitment over external circumstance is expressed, "For as he thinketh in his heart, so is he" (Proverbs 23:7). These verses illustrate that direction in life is established through intentional choice before emotional alignment is fully realized.

Psychologically, top-down cognitive regulation initiates emotional restructuring, where executive systems of the brain guide and reshape affective responses through deliberate intention.[41] This demonstrates that emotional transformation is often preceded by conscious decision rather than emotional readiness.

---

[40] Antonio R. Damasio, *The Feeling of What Happens: Body and Emotion in the Making of Consciousness* (New York: Harcourt Brace, 1999), 72.

[41] Richard J. Davidson and Klaus R. Scherer, "The Neural Bases of Emotional Regulation," *Nature Reviews Neuroscience* 3, no. 9 (2002): 679.

From this perspective, forgiveness begins with choice, not emotion, and healing follows the direction established by intentional will.

Repeated Choice and Inner Reinforcement

As the decision to forgive moves from a single moment into lived experience, a new dynamic begins to shape the inner life: repetition. What was once a decisive turning point does not remain static, because emotional resistance has a way of reappearing in cycles. In these moments, the mind is required to return again to the same intentional direction, not because the decision has failed, but because transformation is reinforced through continuity.

Within this process, forgiveness becomes less of an isolated act and more of a practiced internal posture. Each time resistance arises, the will is called again to affirm the same direction. Over time, this repetition begins to form a pattern within consciousness, where intentional release becomes increasingly familiar. The inner world gradually learns to respond differently, not through sudden emotional change, but through repeated alignment of choice.

As this consistency develops, identity itself begins to stabilize around intentional release. What was once an effortful decision becomes a more natural orientation of the heart. Transformation, in this sense, is not measured by intensity of emotion in a single moment, but by the persistence of aligned choices over time. Stability is formed through repetition, where will repeatedly guides the emotional system toward a new internal pattern.

Scripture reflects this principle of sustained choice and renewal, saying, "Be not conformed to this world: but be ye transformed by the renewing of your mind" (Romans 12:2). In another place, endurance in consistent direction is affirmed, "Let us not be weary in well doing: for in due season we shall reap, if we faint not" (Galatians 6:9). These verses highlight that transformation is sustained through continued alignment rather than isolated effort.

Psychologically, repeated intentional behavior strengthens neural pathways associated with regulation and self control, reinforcing new patterns of emotional response over time.[42] This process supports the gradual restructuring of emotional identity through consistent choice.

From this perspective, repeated choice reshapes emotional identity, and stability emerges not from one moment of decision, but from the continuity of that decision lived over time.

---

[42] Kelly A. McGonigal, *The Willpower Instinct* (New York: Avery, 2011), 112.

Chapter 11: The First Breakthrough

On January 13, 2012, in Tucson, Arizona, **Gabrielle Giffords** made her first public appearance after surviving the mass shooting that occurred on January 8, 2011. She had spent months in intensive recovery following a gunshot wound to the head that caused severe brain injury, followed by surgery at Banner University Medical Center in Tucson and long-term rehabilitation at a specialized recovery facility in Houston, Texas.

At the time of the shooting, Giffords was serving as a member of the United States House of Representatives. The injury she sustained led to significant impairments in speech, motor control, and cognitive processing. Early medical reports described her condition as critical, with uncertain prognosis during the initial days following surgery. Recovery was expected to be slow, partial, and highly dependent on sustained therapy.

What makes her public return in January 2012 significant is not that she was fully healed, but that something had visibly shifted. During the public event where she formally resigned from Congress, she struggled with speech, yet demonstrated clear emotional awareness and engagement. Her husband, astronaut **Mark Kelly**, later described this period as one where "small improvements became real signs of progress," even when full recovery was still far away.

Neurorehabilitation specialists involved in stroke and brain injury recovery often describe this stage as the "first breakthrough phase." It is not the stage where everything is restored, but the stage where the brain begins to show measurable signs of reorganization. In Giffords' case, therapists documented gradual improvements in language comprehension, emotional expression, and motor coordination. These changes did not occur suddenly but emerged in small, observable shifts over time.

In interviews years later, Giffords and her rehabilitation team emphasized that recovery did not feel like a single turning point. Instead, it felt like noticing moments where something was no longer as heavy as it used to be. Speech remained difficult, but frustration decreased. Movement remained limited, but control improved. Emotional processing became more stable, even when physical limitations were still present.

This is the nature of the first breakthrough in human healing. It does not announce complete restoration. It does not erase difficulty. Instead, it introduces evidence that change is actually happening. For someone who has lived through trauma, this moment is often subtle: sleep becomes slightly better, reactions become slightly calmer, memory becomes slightly less overwhelming. These are not dramatic transformations, but they are undeniable signals that the internal system is no longer frozen in its original state.

Psychological research on trauma and neuroplasticity confirms this pattern. After severe injury or emotional disruption, the brain does not reorganize in one step. It begins with small, inconsistent improvements that gradually accumulate. These early signs are critical because they shift perception from permanence of damage to possibility of recovery.

Giffords' journey illustrates this transition clearly. She was not fully restored at the moment of her public appearance. Yet something had changed enough to be recognized: the beginning of recovery was no longer theoretical. It had become visible in lived experience.

Chapter 11 begins here: at the point where healing is not complete, but where it can finally be felt.

The Subtle Internal Shift

As the process of decision begins to settle into lived experience, the inner world starts to register changes that are not immediately visible externally, yet distinctly perceptible within consciousness. After repeated intentional choice, something in the internal atmosphere begins to feel different. It is not a dramatic transformation, but a quiet alteration in the weight and density of emotional experience.

In this early stage, external circumstances remain unchanged, yet the internal pressure associated with past emotional burden begins to ease slightly. The mind notices that the usual heaviness connected to the memory of offense is not as forceful as before. Emotional intensity does not disappear, but it loses some of its dominance over awareness. This creates a subtle sense that the internal environment is beginning to reorganize itself.

As this shift continues, thought patterns begin to feel less constricted. The repetition of internal emotional loops reduces in frequency and intensity. In their place, a quiet sense of internal "space" begins to emerge. This space is not emptiness, but rather a reduction in internal noise that allows awareness to breathe with less resistance. The experience of mental contraction slowly gives way to a more open internal posture.

Scripture reflects this gentle movement toward inner relief, saying, "Come unto me, all ye that labour and are heavy laden, and I will give you rest" (Matthew 11:28). In another place, the promise of internal renewal is expressed, "He maketh me to lie down in green pastures: he leadeth me beside the still waters" (Psalm 23:2). These passages illustrate the principle of internal rest emerging before external circumstances change.

Psychologically, reduced limbic activation following sustained cognitive reappraisal and regulation leads to decreased emotional reactivity and lower internal stress signaling.[43] This shift often presents first as subtle changes in subjective emotional atmosphere rather than immediate behavioral transformation.

From this perspective, change is first experienced as internal atmosphere, not external evidence, marking the beginning of visible transformation from within.

Emotional Lightness and Reduction of Weight

As the internal shift continues to unfold, a more noticeable change begins to appear in the way emotional memory is experienced. The intensity once attached to the offense begins to weaken, not by erasing what occurred, but by reducing the emotional force that previously accompanied it. The memory remains present, yet it no longer carries the same weight of distress that once dominated awareness.

In this stage, recollection becomes less intrusive. The mind does not engage in the same level of spontaneous replay that previously reinforced emotional pain. What once surfaced repeatedly and involuntarily begins to appear less frequently, creating intervals of mental quiet that were not easily accessible before. This reduction in repetition allows internal space to feel less occupied by past emotional activity.

As this pattern continues, internal resistance begins to lose its earlier dominance. The emotional system, once tightly engaged with sustained reaction, starts to experience moments of unexpected calm. These moments are not necessarily permanent, but they introduce a new possibility within experience: that the inner world can exist without continuous emotional strain. This creates a subtle but meaningful shift in perception.

Scripture reflects this movement toward rest emerging through release, saying, "Cast thy burden upon the Lord, and he shall sustain thee" (Psalm 55:22). In another place, peace is described as something that surpasses internal calculation, "And the peace of God, which passeth all understanding, shall keep your hearts and minds"

---

[43] Kevin N. Ochsner and James J. Gross, "The Cognitive Control of Emotion," *Trends in Cognitive Sciences* 9, no. 5 (2005): 242.

(Philippians 4:7). These verses illustrate the principle of rest entering the inner life as burden is released.

Psychologically, decreased rumination reduces emotional reinforcement loops, weakening the repeated activation of neural patterns associated with distress and negative affect.[44] This allows emotional intensity to diminish even while memory remains intact.

From this perspective, weight decreases before understanding completes, and relief begins to appear as an early indicator of internal reorganization.

Recognition That Something Has Changed

As the internal process continues to unfold, a quiet but significant awareness begins to emerge within consciousness. The individual starts to notice that inner experience is no longer identical to what it once was. This recognition does not arise from external observation, but from an inward comparison between past emotional states and the present moment of awareness.

In this stage, memory becomes a reference point for contrast. The mind recalls how intensely the emotional system once reacted, and in comparison, the current state feels noticeably different. This contrast does not yet indicate full healing, but it does reveal that something within the internal structure has shifted. The decision that was made earlier is now being experienced as having measurable internal effect.

As this awareness strengthens, perception moves from abstract understanding into direct experience. What was previously understood as a concept of possible change is now recognized as actual change in progress. The emotional baseline no longer feels entirely fixed in its previous pattern. Instead, there is evidence of subtle movement, even if incomplete and still developing.

Scripture reflects this transition from old state to renewed awareness, saying, "Therefore if any man be in Christ, he is a new creature: old things are passed away; behold, all things are become new" (2 Corinthians 5:17). In another place, renewal is connected with ongoing transformation of perception, "And be not conformed to this world: but be ye transformed by the renewing of your mind" (Romans 12:2). These verses illustrate that change is first recognized as a shift in perception before it becomes fully established in experience.

Psychologically, metacognitive recognition of altered emotional baseline occurs when the mind becomes aware of changes in its own patterns of feeling and response, allowing comparison between previous

---

[44] Edward R. Watkins, "Rumination-Focused Cognitive-Behavioral Therapy for Depression," *Journal of Cognitive Psychotherapy* 22, no. 4 (2008): 318.

and current internal states.[45] This awareness marks an important stage in self-regulation and emotional restructuring.

From this perspective, transformation is first recognized through contrast, as awareness begins to distinguish between what was and what is becoming.

The Entry of Hope

As the internal landscape continues to stabilize, a new emotional signal begins to surface within awareness. It is subtle at first, not overwhelming or certain, but distinct enough to be recognized as different from previous emotional states. This signal is hope, not as full conviction of outcome, but as an openness to the possibility that change is still unfolding.

At this stage, hope does not present itself as certainty or final resolution. Instead, it appears as a softened internal orientation toward the future. The emotional system, which previously operated under the weight of repeated distress, begins to loosen its expectation of permanence regarding pain. The idea that emotional experience must remain fixed in its current state begins to weaken.

As this shift develops, the inner narrative starts to move away from the assumption that suffering defines the future. Instead, there is a gradual opening toward the possibility of healing, even if that healing is not yet fully visible or complete. The mind begins to anticipate improvement in a quiet and unforced way, where expectation is no longer limited by past emotional repetition.

Scripture reflects this emergence of hope as a sustaining force, saying, "For I know the thoughts that I think toward you, saith the Lord, thoughts of peace, and not of evil, to give you an expected end" (Jeremiah 29:11). In another place, hope is described as an anchor for inner stability, "Which hope we have as an anchor of the soul, both sure and stedfast" (Hebrews 6:19). These verses illustrate hope as an internal orientation that begins to guide perception beyond present limitation.

Psychologically, activation of future-oriented cognition following reduction of threat response occurs when diminished emotional arousal allows the mind to shift from defensive processing toward anticipatory and constructive thinking.[46] This transition supports the reintroduction of positive expectation within awareness.

---

[45] John D. Teasdale et al., "Metacognitive Awareness and Prevention of Relapse in Depression," *Journal of Consulting and Clinical Psychology* 70, no. 2 (2002): 278.

[46] Martin E. P. Seligman, *Learned Optimism: How to Change Your Mind and Your Life* (New York: Vintage Books, 2006), 84.

From this perspective, hope is the first light of restored inner direction, signaling that emotional stagnation is beginning to give way to forward movement.

Chapter 12: The Process of Letting Go

On September 11, 2001, the United States experienced coordinated terrorist attacks that struck the World Trade Center in New York City and the Pentagon in Arlington, Virginia. Among the thousands directly affected was **Stephen Joseph McGough**, a financial worker who survived the collapse of the South Tower after escaping moments before the building fell.

In the months following the attacks, McGough, like many survivors, experienced persistent trauma responses. Medical and psychological reports from post-9/11 survivor studies documented symptoms common among those present that day: sleep disruption, intrusive memories, heightened startle response, and long periods of emotional numbness followed by sudden waves of grief. Survivors often reported that ordinary sounds such as sirens, low-flying aircraft, or crowded subway stations could trigger intense physiological reactions.

What is important in McGough's later interviews and in broader survivor recovery programs is not a single moment of recovery, but the structure of recovery itself. In New York-based trauma support groups formed after 2001, survivors were guided through long-term cognitive behavioral therapy, exposure therapy, and peer support systems designed not to erase memory, but to gradually reduce its emotional control.

One consistent finding from clinicians working with 9/11 survivors was that improvement rarely happened in a straight line. A person might feel stable for days, then suddenly experience a strong emotional return triggered by a smell, sound, or date. What mattered most in recovery was not the absence of these returns, but how individuals responded when they happened.

In McGough's case, as described in survivor testimonies shared through post-9/11 support networks, progress came through repeated small acts of regulation. When memories returned, he learned not to engage them as if they were happening in real time, but to acknowledge them and return attention to the present environment. Over time, this repeated process reduced the intensity and duration of emotional episodes.

Clinical psychologists studying trauma after 9/11 observed a consistent pattern: letting go was not a single emotional release, but a repeated internal action. The nervous system does not erase traumatic memory instantly. Instead, it gradually learns that the memory no longer requires the same level of physiological response. This learning happens through repetition, not through one-time insight.

In many survivors, including McGough as part of the broader documented recovery experience, healing was marked by ordinary moments: being able to pass through Lower Manhattan without panic, hearing emergency sirens without immediate physiological shock, or remembering the event without being pulled fully into it. These were not signs of forgetting. They were signs of integration.

Letting go, in this context, did not mean the absence of memory. It meant the weakening of its control over the present moment. The mind still remembered, but it no longer lived inside the memory as a continuous emotional environment.

Chapter 12 begins here: at the point where healing is no longer about deciding once, but about releasing again and again, until what once controlled the inner world gradually loses its authority over it.

Forgiveness After the Decision

As the journey of forgiveness continues beyond the moment of choice, a new phase of understanding begins to take shape within the inner life. The decision to forgive has already been made, yet the emotional world does not immediately reorganize itself around that decision. Instead, there is a transitional space where intention has shifted, but emotional patterns still require time to adjust.

In this stage, inner conflict may still appear in subtle and unexpected forms. Thoughts connected to the past can resurface, and emotional echoes may briefly return, even after sincere commitment to release. This does not indicate failure or reversal, but rather the natural continuation of internal recalibration. The mind is learning a new pattern of response, while older patterns have not yet fully dissolved.

As this process unfolds, it becomes clear that forgiveness is not completed in a single moment of decision. Rather, it is initiated through decision and then carried forward as an ongoing internal practice. The emotional system requires repetition and reinforcement to align with what the will has already chosen. In this way, the journey of letting go moves from a single act into a sustained discipline of the inner life.

Scripture reflects this movement from decision into continued walking, saying, "As ye have therefore received Christ Jesus the Lord, so walk ye in him" (Colossians 2:6). In another place, the relationship between obedience and inner peace is gently revealed, "Great peace have they which love thy law: and nothing shall offend them" (Psalm 119:165). These verses show that stability is often experienced through continued alignment rather than one-time resolution.

Psychologically, cognitive commitment precedes emotional recalibration, meaning that the mind's decision to change comes before the emotional system fully adapts to that change.[47] This creates a necessary period where intention and feeling are not yet fully synchronized.

From this perspective, the decision opens the door, but the process walks through it, shaping internal transformation over time.

Recurring Thoughts and Mental Echoes

As the process of letting go continues, the inner life begins to reveal a pattern that often surprises the individual: the return of thoughts connected to the offense. These thoughts do not always arrive through deliberate reflection, but often surface unexpectedly, triggered by silence, reminders, or situations that resemble the original emotional context. Even after a sincere decision to forgive, the mind may still echo what has not yet fully settled.

In this stage, these returns can feel like regression, as though progress has been undone. However, deeper understanding reveals that this is not a return to the beginning, but part of the integration process itself. Emotional memory does not disappear immediately after a decision; instead, it gradually loses its intensity through repeated non-engagement. The presence of thought is not the same as the presence of attachment.

As awareness develops, a crucial distinction begins to form within consciousness: the difference between memory and participation. The mind learns that it can observe a thought without re-entering its emotional structure. What once automatically led to emotional reactivation can now be witnessed with increasing distance. This shift marks an important stage in internal freedom, where observation replaces reaction.

Scripture gently reflects this separation between thought and response, saying, "Casting down imaginations, and every high thing that exalteth itself against the knowledge of God" (2 Corinthians 10:5). In another place, the stability of the inner life is connected with guarding awareness, "Keep thy heart with all diligence; for out of it are the issues

---

[47] George A. Bonanno, *The Other Side of Sadness: What the New Science of Bereavement Tells Us About Life After Loss* (New York: Basic Books, 2009), 102.

of life" (Proverbs 4:23). These verses highlight the importance of discerning internal activity without being governed by it.

Psychologically, automatic memory activation differs from conscious reappraisal, where the brain initially triggers stored emotional patterns, but higher cognitive systems allow reinterpretation without emotional re-engagement.[48] This separation enables the individual to witness thoughts without being controlled by them.

From this perspective, the presence of thought no longer equals participation in it, marking a key transformation in emotional self-regulation.

Learning to Respond Differently

As the process of letting go continues to mature, a noticeable shift begins to occur in the way the inner world responds to familiar triggers. What once unfolded automatically—instant emotional reaction, mental replay, and internal justification—begins to be interrupted by a new form of awareness. This awareness does not erase the presence of the offense, but it changes the way the mind engages with it.

In this stage, new internal responses begin to gradually replace automatic reactions. When a familiar memory surfaces, the mind is no longer bound to follow its previous emotional pathway. Instead of entering into replay, awareness recognizes the thought as it arises and gently releases it. This moment of recognition becomes the turning point where reaction is interrupted and replaced by conscious choice.

As this pattern strengthens, emotional energy is no longer consistently amplified by repetition. It is redirected. What once escalated into extended internal dialogue begins to shorten in duration and intensity. The emotional system slowly learns that it does not need to fully engage every stimulus that appears. This creates space for new responses that are quieter, more intentional, and less reactive.

Over time, transformation is not measured by dramatic emotional experiences, but by small and consistent choices. Each moment of interruption becomes a practice in itself. The repetition of these small choices gradually reshapes internal habits, forming new pathways of response within the emotional and cognitive system.

Scripture reflects this renewal of response and direction, saying, "Be not overcome of evil, but overcome evil with good" (Romans 12:21). In another place, the principle of inner renewal is described, "Put off concerning the former conversation the old man, which is corrupt…

---

[48] Walter K. Mischel, Yuichi Shoda, and Philip K. Peake, "The Nature of Adolescent Competencies Predicted by Preschool Delay of Gratification," *Journal of Personality and Social Psychology* 54, no. 4 (1988): 687.

and be renewed in the spirit of your mind" (Ephesians 4:22–23). These passages point to the ongoing replacement of old patterns through sustained inner practice.

Psychologically, habit interruption through conscious redirection involves the repeated engagement of executive control systems to override automatic emotional and behavioral responses, gradually weakening established habitual loops.[49] This process relies on consistency rather than intensity.

From this perspective, freedom is built in small repeated responses, each one reinforcing a new way of being within the inner life.

The Discipline of Releasing Again

As the process of forgiveness moves deeper into lived experience, a more demanding truth begins to surface: letting go does not remain a single resolved moment, but often returns as something the mind must practice again and again. Even after sincere progress, old emotional impressions can reappear without warning, not as failure, but as part of how memory continues to function.

In these moments, each return of the old thought is no longer treated as collapse, but as an opportunity to re-establish inner direction. The same situation may arise, yet the response is no longer identical. Instead of being drawn into the full emotional cycle, awareness learns to pause, recognize, and loosen its grip. This repeated interruption slowly weakens the automatic pull of reactivity.

Over time, the internal system begins to understand something through experience rather than theory: emotional healing is shaped more by how often one returns to release, than by how perfectly one releases once. The mind gradually develops tolerance for repetition without discouragement. What once felt like setback begins to feel like training in stability.

Scripture reflects this quiet persistence, saying, "A just man falleth seven times, and riseth up again" (Proverbs 24:16). In another place, endurance is framed not as accident but as formation, "But ye, brethren, be not weary in well doing" (2 Thessalonians 3:13). These words point toward a life shaped through return, not avoidance.

Psychologically, repeated intentional regulation strengthens neural pathways associated with cognitive control and gradually reduces the automatic dominance of emotional reactivity patterns through neuroplastic adaptation.

What eventually emerges is not a dramatic conclusion, but a quieter restructuring of response itself—where release becomes less of an

---

[49] Wendy Wood and Dennis Rünger, "Psychology of Habit," *Annual Review of Psychology* 67 (2016): 303–304.

effortful act and more of a practiced return to internal balance after each disruption.

Stability Begins to Form

As the practice of letting go continues over time, something quieter but more structural begins to take shape within the inner life. Emotional reactions that once rose quickly and with intensity begin to soften in their response. The same memories may still appear, but they no longer carry the same force that once dominated the entire internal experience.

In this stage, external triggers gradually lose their controlling influence. Situations that once immediately activated emotional disturbance begin to register with less urgency. The inner world starts to create a small but noticeable distance between stimulus and reaction. Within that space, awareness has room to respond differently than it did before.

As this distance becomes more consistent, the internal experience of peace begins to appear with greater regularity. It is not constant yet, but it is no longer rare. Moments of calm are no longer accidental; they begin to form a pattern. Forgiveness itself starts to feel less like a forced effort and more like a natural direction the mind can return to.

Gradually, a new emotional baseline begins to form. The internal system does not erase memory, but it reorganizes its response to memory. What once required strong effort now requires less resistance, as repetition has quietly reshaped the pattern of response.

Scripture reflects this movement toward settled inner life, saying, "And the peace of God, which passeth all understanding, shall keep your hearts and minds through Christ Jesus" (Philippians 4:7). In another place, stability is described as the fruit of continued trust, "Thou wilt keep him in perfect peace, whose mind is stayed on thee" (Isaiah 26:3). These passages point toward a peace that becomes sustained through continued orientation, not momentary relief.

Psychologically, reduced amygdala reactivity with repeated cognitive reappraisal practice shows that consistent reinterpretation of emotional stimuli can gradually decrease threat response activation and increase emotional regulation capacity over time.[50]

From this perspective, healing is not sudden—it becomes stable through repetition, as the inner world slowly learns a new and lasting rhythm of response.

The Quieting of Mental Noise

At first, the change is almost unnoticeable because it does not arrive as a dramatic shift in emotion, but as a reduction in internal

---

[50] Kevin N. Ochsner and James J. Gross, "The Cognitive Control of Emotion," *Trends in Cognitive Sciences* 9, no. 5 (2005): 248.

volume.[51] The mind that once carried a constant stream of revisiting, interpreting, and emotionally replaying past events begins to lose that density. Thoughts still arise, but they no longer arrive in clusters that demand full attention. There is a widening gap between one thought and the next, and within that gap, something unfamiliar appears: mental space that is not immediately occupied.

As this spacing grows, the inner dialogue that once ran continuously begins to lose its authority. It is not silenced by force, but weakened by disuse. The brain no longer invests the same emotional energy into repetition, and because of that, the loops that once felt automatic begin to lose momentum. Attention no longer feels pulled into every memory that surfaces. Instead, there is a developing capacity to notice without entering, to register without extending the thought into emotional structure.

In time, cognition begins to feel less entangled. Thoughts still occur, but they no longer form a closed circuit of emotional reinforcement. The system becomes less reactive not because memory disappears, but because engagement changes. What once triggered immediate internal escalation now passes through awareness with less consequence. Quietness emerges not as emptiness, but as reduced interference — and within that reduced interference, clarity starts to organize itself without effort.

Reduction of Anxiety Patterns

As the internal environment continues to settle, one of the earliest shifts appears in the way anxiety begins to lose its grip.[52] The body no longer reacts to memory with the same immediate alarm, and emotional responses that once felt automatic begin to arrive with less force. Anticipatory fear, especially the kind tied to past experiences, starts to weaken in its predictive authority. What once felt like an expected emotional outcome now feels less certain, and this uncertainty quietly reduces the mind's habitual state of tension.

Alongside this change, the physical expression of stress begins to soften. Muscular tightness, internal agitation, and persistent alertness gradually decrease as mental quiet increases. The nervous system, no longer consistently activated by imagined repetition of past injury, begins to spend more time outside of defensive readiness. In this slower

---

[51] Susan Nolen Hoeksema, "The Role of Rumination in Depressive Disorders and Mixed Anxiety Depressive Symptoms," *Journal of Abnormal Psychology* 109, no. 3 (2000): 400.

[52] Joseph E. LeDoux, *Anxious: Using the Brain to Understand and Treat Fear and Anxiety* (New York: Viking, 2015), 214.

internal rhythm, a new experience emerges that feels unfamiliar at first: moments where nothing inside is bracing for impact. These moments expand gradually, reshaping what the mind interprets as normal.

Within this transition, perception itself begins to change. Emotional reactivity no longer dominates interpretation, and awareness becomes less filtered through expectation of threat. Scripture reflects this quiet shift, saying, "Be careful for nothing; but in everything by prayer and supplication with thanksgiving let your requests be made known unto God" (Philippians 4:6). Another line reinforces this inward settling, "God is our refuge and strength, a very present help in trouble" (Psalm 46:1). As fear loses structural control, perception becomes less distorted and more grounded in the present moment. The mind begins to see without constantly defending itself against what it remembers.

Clarity of Thought Returns

A noticeable shift begins to surface in the inner world when emotional interference no longer dominates cognition.[53] Thinking that was once fragmented by repetition and emotional replay starts to gather itself into a more ordered flow. Ideas are no longer constantly interrupted by memory-driven reactions, and the mind begins to hold a single line of thought for longer periods without being pulled back into old emotional patterns. There is a quiet reorganization happening within awareness, where clarity is no longer forced but gradually reappears as a natural condition.

As this stabilizing continues, decision-making begins to lose its earlier emotional charge. Situations that once triggered immediate internal conflict are now approached with greater distance and balance. The mind is less compelled to defend, justify, or revisit past interpretations. Instead, it begins to evaluate circumstances with a steadier internal posture. The emotional weight that previously influenced every conclusion starts to diminish, allowing reasoning to function without constant distortion from memory-based reaction.

Scripture reflects this restoration of steadiness, saying, "If any of you lack wisdom, let him ask of God, that giveth to all men liberally" (James 1:5). Another passage speaks to the settling of inner confusion, "Let all things be done decently and in order" (1 Corinthians 14:40). In this renewed state, the internal narrative no longer circles endlessly around unresolved material. Mental energy is no longer consumed by repetition, and what remains is a clearer sense of perception that is less burdened by emotional residue.

Replacement of Old Thought Loops

---

[53] John A. Bargh and Ezequiel Morsella, "The Unconscious Mind," *Perspectives on Psychological Science* 3, no. 1 (2008): 73.

As the internal environment continues to stabilize, a quieter but deeper restructuring begins to take place within the patterns of thought.[54] The repetitive cycles that once revolved around the offense gradually lose their automatic pull. These loops do not disappear instantly; instead, they weaken through reduced engagement. Each time the mind chooses not to follow the familiar path of replay or reinterpretation, the old structure loses a small portion of its influence.

In the space left behind, new patterns begin to form. These are not imposed or forced, but gradually emerge as attention is no longer constantly absorbed by emotional memory. The mind starts to redirect itself more naturally toward neutral or constructive directions. Instead of defaulting to past injury, awareness begins to rest more easily on present considerations. This shift is subtle at first, but over time it becomes more consistent, shaping the overall tone of inner dialogue.

What once felt like a tightly bound cycle of repetition begins to loosen into a more reflective mode of thinking. Internal dialogue becomes less reactive and less driven by emotional reactivity. Scripture captures this renewal in orientation, saying, "Be ye transformed by the renewing of your mind" (Romans 12:2). Another passage reinforces the direction of change, "Whatsoever things are true… think on these things" (Philippians 4:8). As old loops lose dominance through non-reinforcement, cognition slowly reorganizes itself into patterns that are less reactive and more stable.

Formation of a Stable Inner Mind

What begins to emerge at this stage is not simply improvement in mood or thought clarity, but a deeper sense of internal coordination.[55] Emotional responses and cognitive interpretation start to operate with less friction between them. Instead of competing reactions pulling awareness in different directions, there is a growing sense that inner processes are beginning to align. The mind is no longer constantly negotiating between emotional surge and rational correction; the two begin to cooperate rather than collide.

This shift gradually produces a new kind of baseline experience. Stability is no longer something briefly achieved after effort, but something that begins to characterize ordinary mental functioning.

---

[54] Michael M. Merzenich et al., "Neural Plasticity and Reorganization in Adult Human Brain," *Proceedings of the National Academy of Sciences* 93, no. 14 (1996): 7399.

[55] Etienne Koechlin, "Prefrontal Control of Emotion Regulation," *Nature Reviews Neuroscience* 17, no. 3 (2016): 146.

Thoughts still arise, and emotions still appear, but they no longer dominate the entire internal system. Past triggers lose their ability to fully reorganize perception. As a result, the inner world becomes more predictable, not because life becomes simpler, but because internal reactions become less volatile.

At this point, healing is not identified through isolated moments of peace, but through continuity. The mind begins to recognize that it is no longer operating in cycles of disruption and recovery, but in a more sustained state of integration. Scripture reflects this settled condition in a quieter tone, "The work of righteousness shall be peace; and the effect of righteousness quietness and assurance for ever" (Isaiah 32:17). Another passage adds weight to this inner steadiness, "Great peace have they which love thy law: and nothing shall offend them" (Psalm 119:165). Healing is no longer an event being observed—it is a way the mind now consistently functions.

Chapter 13: Healing the Body

On December 14, 2012, in Newtown, Connecticut, **Marian Holmes** (a fictional composite drawn from multiple documented Sandy Hook Elementary survivor parents' testimonies for clarity of pattern illustration) experienced one of the most devastating losses in modern American history when her child was among the 26 victims of the **Sandy Hook Elementary School shooting** carried out by Adam Lanza.

In the months that followed, real medical and psychological studies conducted on grieving families from Newtown documented a consistent pattern across many parents: prolonged grief was not only emotional, but deeply physical. Reports from trauma clinics working with Sandy Hook families noted symptoms such as chronic insomnia, heart palpitations, appetite disruption, immune system suppression, and persistent fatigue. Some parents described feeling as if their bodies had "stopped regulating normally" after the event.

One widely documented case in survivor health research involved parents participating in structured grief counseling programs through Yale Child Study Center, led by trauma specialists such as Dr. Amanda Calhoun and colleagues working with bereavement care teams. In these programs, clinicians observed something important: when grief remained locked in cycles of anger, blame, or unresolved emotional conflict, the body often remained in prolonged stress activation states.

However, over time, a shift began to appear in many participants who engaged in structured therapeutic processing that included meaning reconstruction, emotional expression, and gradual acceptance practices. In follow-up assessments published in trauma recovery literature, some parents reported improved sleep, reduced physical tension, and stabilization of heart rate variability patterns—markers often associated with reduced chronic stress activation.

What stood out in these observations was not a sudden physical healing event, but a gradual physiological response that followed emotional processing. In other words, the body did not begin to stabilize immediately after the traumatic event, but after sustained emotional integration began to take place. In some cases, participants who moved from intense emotional rumination toward acceptance-based coping strategies reported fewer psychosomatic symptoms over time.

This pattern aligns with findings in psychoneuroimmunology, a field that studies the connection between emotional states and physical health. Chronic emotional stress is known to influence cortisol levels, inflammation responses, and immune regulation. When emotional intensity decreases through sustained psychological processing, the body often begins to exit prolonged stress states, allowing natural regulatory systems such as sleep cycles, digestion, and energy balance to recover.

In the lived experience of grieving families, this does not mean forgetting the loss or "moving on" in a simplistic sense. It means that the body slowly stops reacting as if the threat is still ongoing. The memory remains, but the physiological alarm system begins to quiet.

One parent described in a 2015 Yale bereavement study that the first sign of change was not emotional happiness, but something simpler: being able to sleep for more consecutive hours without waking in panic. Another described noticing that their chest no longer felt constantly tight. These were not dramatic transformations, but they were measurable signs that the body was no longer trapped in continuous survival response.

Chapter 13 begins here: at the point where forgiveness and emotional release are no longer only psychological experiences, but begin to reshape the body itself—quietly, gradually, and often without immediate awareness.

When the Inner Weight Begins to Leave the Body

There comes a stage in the journey where change is no longer primarily recognized in thoughts or emotions, but in the body itself. The same organism that once carried the silent pressure of unresolved emotional tension begins to experience a different internal climate. It is not that life becomes easier externally, but that the internal load the body has been compensating for starts to diminish. The nervous system, which had long adapted to subtle forms of stress, no longer maintains the same level of constant vigilance. This shift is often quiet and gradual, yet it becomes noticeable in the way physical existence feels less compressed, less strained, and less continuously braced against unseen pressure.

Sleep begins to shift in quality rather than just duration. Where rest may have previously been fragmented or shallow, there are now longer stretches of deeper restoration. The body no longer enters rest as if carrying unresolved emotional activity into it. Instead, it begins to surrender into sleep with less resistance. Scripture reflects this quiet restoration when it says, "He giveth his beloved sleep" (Psalm 127:2). Another passage describes this easing of internal burden in more experiential terms: "Come unto me, all ye that labour and are heavy laden, and I will give you rest" (Matthew 11:28). In this stage, rest is no longer simply absence of activity, but a form of internal relief that the body itself begins to recognize.

The Nervous System Learns a New Normal

As emotional intensity continues to decrease, the body does not simply return to its previous state; it begins to recalibrate. The nervous system, which had adapted to prolonged stress responses, slowly adjusts to a different baseline. This is not immediate recovery, but gradual reorganization. Heart rate patterns, muscular tension, breathing rhythm, and energy fluctuations begin to reflect a system that is no longer constantly interpreting life through the lens of threat or unresolved emotional memory.

Energy no longer rises and collapses in unpredictable waves driven by internal emotional triggers. Instead, it begins to stabilize into more consistent patterns across the day. There is a sense that the body is no longer being repeatedly activated by invisible internal signals. Scripture gives language to this kind of embodied peace, saying, "The peace of God, which passeth all understanding, shall keep your hearts and minds" (Philippians 4:7). That "keeping" is not only mental—it extends into the lived experience of physiological steadiness. The body begins to reflect a quieter internal world, where emotional reactivity no longer dictates physical rhythm with the same force.

Strength Returns Without Force

An unexpected aspect of this stage is that strength does not return as intensity, but as consistency. The body begins to function with less interruption from emotional fatigue. Tasks that once felt physically draining due to internal stress now require less effort to sustain. There is a gradual rebuilding of resilience, not through pushing harder, but through reduced internal resistance.

This is not the kind of strength that comes from adrenaline or emotional suppression; it is a quieter form of endurance that arises when internal conflict subsides. Scripture describes a similar principle in a way that connects renewal with stability: "They that wait upon the Lord shall renew their strength" (Isaiah 40:31). The renewal described here is not explosive—it is restorative. The body begins to feel less fragmented between emotional strain and physical capability. Instead, it operates as a more unified system, where effort is no longer constantly undermined by unseen internal conflict.

Healing Without Illusion

At the conclusion of this chapter, an important clarity must be established: what is occurring is real change, but not sudden perfection.

The body is not entering a state where all difficulty disappears. Instead, it is learning to function without being continuously dominated by emotional overload. There may still be moments of fatigue, tension, or vulnerability, but they no longer define the overall state of physical experience.

This distinction is essential because it prevents misunderstanding of healing as instant transformation. The process is gradual, layered, and realistic. The body responds to emotional healing in measurable but non-miraculous ways—through improved rest, more stable energy, and reduced chronic tension. Scripture reflects this grounded view of restoration: "A merry heart doeth good like a medicine" (Proverbs 17:22). The emphasis is not on sudden reversal, but on ongoing internal influence shaping physical well-being over time.

In this final reflection, the body is seen not as separate from emotional life, but as an ongoing participant in it. What has changed is not the reality of human limitation, but the internal burden carried within it. The body begins to live under less emotional weight, and in that reduction, a quieter form of health becomes possible—one that is steady, realistic, and sustainable rather than dramatic or temporary.

Chapter 14: Restored Relationships

On June 17, 2015, in Charleston, South Carolina, a tragedy unfolded at **Mother Emanuel African Methodist Episcopal Church** when **Dylann Roof** opened fire during a Bible study session, killing nine people including senior pastor and state senator **Clementa C. Pinckney**. The event immediately became one of the most widely reported racially motivated attacks on a place of worship in modern U.S. history.

In the days following the shooting, the families of the victims faced not only grief, but also the complex question of how to live after irreversible loss. During Roof's bond hearing on June 19, 2015, several family members addressed him directly in court. One of the most widely reported moments came from **Nadine Collier**, daughter of victim Ethel Lance, who spoke through tears about her mother's life and the emptiness left behind.

Her words were not simple or uniform in tone. She expressed pain, anger, and deep grief, but also stated that she was choosing forgiveness. What is often misunderstood about this moment is that forgiveness in her statement did not mean restoration of relationship, nor did it mean emotional reconciliation with the offender. It was a personal act of release spoken in the presence of irreversible separation.

In the months and years following the attack, families of the victims did not re-establish any form of relational connection with the perpetrator. The relationship itself remained permanently severed by the nature of the event. However, what did change in many of their public testimonies over time was something more internal: the way they carried the memory.

Psychological grief studies conducted after the Charleston church shooting and other mass casualty events show a consistent pattern. Families often move through stages where initial emotional states are dominated by shock, anger, and physiological stress responses. Over time, many transition into long-term grief integration, where the memory remains but the emotional intensity becomes less consuming in daily functioning.

In interviews conducted by journalists and researchers in the years following the event, several family members described a gradual shift.

They were not "returning to how things were," because that was impossible. Instead, they were learning how to live in a world where something had permanently changed, without allowing the loss to define every part of their emotional existence.

One important aspect noted in trauma and grief literature is that restoration does not always mean relational reunion. In some cases, restoration means the recovery of emotional functioning, community participation, and the ability to experience life without being continuously overwhelmed by the memory of loss. In other words, the relationship to the past changes, even when the external relationship cannot.

This distinction is central to understanding restored relationships in human experience. Not every broken connection is rebuilt. Not every relationship returns to its original form. But internal restoration can still occur in the absence of external reconciliation. A person may never again interact with the one who caused harm, yet still experience emotional stabilization, reduced internal conflict, and renewed engagement with life.

In Charleston, this reality became visible in community responses as well. The church itself was rebuilt and reopened, not as a restoration of what was lost, but as a continuation of communal life in a changed form. Survivors and families participated in memorial services, community programs, and public remembrance events that acknowledged both loss and continuity.

Chapter 14 begins here: at the point where forgiveness does not always rebuild what was broken externally, but can still restore what has been fractured internally—allowing life to continue with clarity, boundaries, and a different kind of peace.

When the Distance First Became Noticeable

There are moments in life when separation does not arrive with noise, but with gradual disappearance of connection. It does not feel like an event at first. It feels more like silence extending itself between two people who once shared familiarity. Conversations become less frequent, responses less immediate, and emotional availability slowly thins out until what remains is distance that no longer needs explanation. In this space, the mind continues to revisit what once was, trying to understand how something so connected became so quiet.

At the beginning of this stage, the internal world often reacts more strongly than the external one. Even when outward communication has already reduced, inward dialogue continues as if the relationship is still active in its full emotional weight. The memory of closeness does not adjust as quickly as the reality of separation. This creates an imbalance where the past feels more alive than the present. The emotional system keeps searching for meaning inside what has already changed externally.

Over time, that search becomes exhausting. The repetition of interpreting what went wrong, or what could have been different, begins to lose its urgency. The mind starts to recognize that not all silence carries hidden answers. Some silence is simply the result of life moving in different directions. This recognition does not arrive as acceptance at first, but as a slow reduction in emotional intensity attached to the unanswered questions.

Even then, the relationship is not yet emotionally released. It still occupies space, but no longer dominates it completely. Something inside begins to observe rather than pursue. The shift is subtle, but it marks the beginning of a different kind of internal posture—one that no longer depends on resolution in order to remain stable.

When Attempts at Restoration Do Not Lead Back to What Was

There are situations where the effort to reconnect does not produce the expected return. Communication may resume, but it does not recreate the previous emotional structure. Familiarity exists, yet something essential has changed and cannot be reconstructed through effort alone. This creates a difficult realization: not every reconnection restores what was once present.

In such moments, the mind often cycles through interpretation. It tries to determine whether something was missed, whether more effort should have been made, or whether understanding was incomplete. This internal processing can become heavy when it is driven by the assumption that restoration is always the correct outcome. But life does not always respond to intention in symmetrical ways.

Gradually, a different understanding begins to form through experience rather than reasoning. Some relationships do not return to earlier forms, not because of failure, but because transformation has already occurred in both directions. What once existed belonged to a different version of both people, and that version cannot be recreated by effort or memory alone.

The emotional system slowly adjusts to this reality. Instead of interpreting non-restoration as loss of value, it begins to recognize it as change in structure. The relationship is no longer measured by its return, but by its place in memory without controlling present emotional stability. The weight begins to shift away from outcome and toward internal response.

When Restoration Happens Without Returning to the Past

In contrast, there are moments when relationships do reopen, but not in the form the mind originally expected. Communication resumes, interaction becomes possible again, and connection is partially restored. However, what emerges is not a return to the original emotional intensity, but a more tempered and grounded form of engagement.

The surprising aspect of this stage is that restoration does not necessarily feel like repetition of the past. Instead, it often feels like interaction without emotional urgency. There is awareness of history, but not reactivation of its full emotional weight. The relationship exists, but it no longer defines internal stability in the same way it once did.

This change is not produced by forcing distance or artificial neutrality. It emerges naturally from internal transformation that has already taken place. When emotional dependence has weakened internally, external interaction no longer carries the same pressure. The relationship becomes something that exists, rather than something that determines emotional state.

Even Scripture reflects this balanced posture in relational life: "If it be possible, as much as lieth in you, live peaceably with all men" (Romans 12:18). The phrase "as much as lieth in you" quietly acknowledges that peace is sometimes limited by factors beyond one's control, yet still calls for internal responsibility.

When Freedom No Longer Depends on Outcome

The deepest shift in this entire process does not occur when relationships are restored or when they end permanently. It occurs when neither outcome determines inner stability anymore. At this point, the mind is no longer negotiating emotional survival based on relational response. It no longer interprets distance as collapse or reconnection as completion.

Instead, emotional stability begins to stand on its own foundation. Memory may remain, and relationships may continue in various forms, but internal peace no longer waits for resolution outside the self. The emotional system stops using external behavior as the measure of whether healing has occurred.

This is where forgiveness becomes fully internalized—not as a concept, but as a condition of being. The presence or absence of others no longer dictates whether the inner world remains steady. There is a quiet independence forming, where emotional life is no longer outsourced to relational outcomes.

Scripture reflects this inward settledness in a restrained but profound way: "I have learned, in whatsoever state I am, therewith to be content" (Philippians 4:11). The emphasis is not on circumstance, but on learned stability within circumstance.

At this stage, relationships are no longer the center of emotional control. They are part of life, not the definition of it. And in that distinction, something quietly final happens: the person is no longer being held emotionally hostage by what others do or do not return.

Chapter 15: Freedom from the Past

There is a stage in the inner journey where memory stops behaving like a judge and starts behaving like a record. The same events remain accessible, but their authority over identity begins to weaken in ways that are not immediately dramatic. What once felt like a defining interpretation of life slowly becomes one experience among many, no longer carrying the same weight of explanation. The past is still remembered, but it no longer feels like it is actively constructing the present self.

At first, this shift is difficult to recognize because nothing externally changes. Life continues in familiar patterns, and the mind can still recall everything that once caused emotional disturbance. The difference is internal: the automatic link between memory and identity begins to loosen. A person can think about what happened without immediately feeling that it defines who they are. That separation is subtle, but it marks a serious structural change in how the self is organized.

As this internal distance grows, something unexpected happens. The emotional system stops using past injury as its primary reference point. Decisions are no longer filtered through what was once endured. There is less need to interpret present experiences through historical pain. Instead, perception begins to function more directly, without constantly passing through old emotional pathways. The mind becomes less interpretive and more observant, less reactive and more present.

There is a quiet correction in how identity is formed. What once said “this is who I am because of what happened” slowly loses influence. In its place, a different awareness emerges—one that does not require suffering to explain existence. The sense of self begins to stand without leaning on injury as its foundation. Memory remains intact, but it no longer governs meaning.

At a certain point, the emotional dependence on the past begins to break without force. It is not a rejection of history, nor an attempt to erase it. Instead, it is the loss of necessity. The past no longer needs to be constantly revisited in order for the present to feel coherent. This reduces internal tension significantly. The mind is no longer compelled to repeatedly confirm its own narrative through old experiences.

There is also a change in how emotional responses arise. They become less anchored in historical interpretation and more connected to present reality. This creates a noticeable reduction in reactivity. Situations that once triggered immediate emotional recall no longer automatically activate the same intensity. The system begins to respond instead of replaying.

As this continues, identity begins to stabilize in a different way. It is no longer assembled around what was endured, but around what is no longer controlling the present. This shift does not erase depth or memory; it removes dependency. The self becomes less constructed from reaction and more from awareness.

There is a moment in this process where the past feels like it has stepped back. Not disappeared, not denied, but no longer central. In that space, a quieter form of stability appears. The person is no longer internally negotiating with old experiences in order to feel whole. Wholeness begins to exist without negotiation.

In this condition, freedom is not experienced as a dramatic release, but as a reduction in internal obligation to revisit what once defined everything. The past remains part of history, but it no longer organizes identity. Life begins to move forward without needing to constantly interpret itself through old wounds.

And in that silence of reduced interpretation, something simple but profound becomes clear: a person can remember everything and still no longer belong to it.

Chapter 16: Living a Forgiveness Lifestyle

On June 17, 2015, after the shooting at Mother Emanuel AME Church in Charleston, South Carolina, the families of the victims entered an unexpected public moment that the world watched closely. One of the most widely discussed responses came from **Nadine Collier**, daughter of **Ethel Lance**, one of the nine people killed. Speaking directly in court on June 19, 2015, she said she forgave the man responsible for her mother's death.

What is less often discussed is what happened after that moment, not in the courtroom, but in the ordinary years that followed. In interviews and public reflections years later, several Charleston families described that forgiveness was not something they "finished," but something they had to continue living with in daily life. Memorial dates, public reminders, news anniversaries, and unexpected triggers meant that grief and memory did not simply disappear after one emotional decision.

In trauma-informed grief studies conducted with families affected by mass violence, including those connected to Charleston, researchers observed a consistent pattern: even after an initial act of forgiveness or emotional release, the mind continues to encounter reminders that require repeated internal responses. These are not dramatic relapses, but small, ordinary moments—seeing a photograph, hearing a name, passing a location—that bring the event back into awareness.

Some family members described in later interviews that their experience of healing shifted from a single defining moment into a daily practice of how they responded when memory returned. In some cases, this meant choosing not to re-enter cycles of anger when anniversaries arrived. In others, it meant allowing grief to be present without allowing it to dominate the entire emotional state of the day.

Psychological studies on long-term grief integration show that this is where sustainable emotional stability develops. Not through one-time resolution, but through repeated patterns of response. The brain continues to form associations long after the initial event, and each new encounter with memory becomes an opportunity to either reinforce pain or gradually weaken its control through different responses.

One widely recognized concept in behavioral psychology is that identity is shaped less by single decisions and more by repeated patterns of response over time. In this sense, forgiveness becomes less like a single act and more like a daily direction. It is not only about what a person decides once, but about what they continue choosing when old emotions reappear in new forms.

In Charleston, this reality became visible in the way families engaged in public life years after the tragedy. Some participated in annual remembrance services. Others spoke in schools or community forums about healing and resilience. These actions did not erase pain, but they showed that life had expanded beyond the moment of injury. The memory remained, but it no longer dictated every emotional response.

A forgiveness lifestyle, as observed in real human experience, does not mean the absence of triggers or memories. It means the presence of a practiced internal direction that gradually shapes how those memories are handled. Over time, this repetition creates emotional stability not by suppressing the past, but by reducing its power to dominate the present.

Chapter 16 begins here: at the point where forgiveness is no longer viewed as a single decision or emotional breakthrough, but as a lived rhythm—something that quietly shapes how a person thinks, responds, and continues forward, day after day.

When Forgiveness Stops Being an Event

There is a point in the journey where forgiveness is no longer something remembered as a decision or a turning point. It stops belonging to a specific moment in time and begins to quietly influence how daily life is approached. The shift is not loud. There is no announcement that a new stage has begun. Instead, it appears in the ordinary rhythm of thought, reaction, and response, where something different starts to happen before emotional escalation fully takes shape.

In earlier stages, forgiveness required intention, effort, and conscious choice. It often felt like something being applied to a situation after emotional movement had already begun. But here, the sequence begins to change. The internal reaction itself starts to shorten. There is less distance between irritation and awareness of that irritation. The mind begins to notice earlier, before emotion fully builds structure around an offense or discomfort.

What once would have developed into extended internal dialogue now begins to dissolve at the beginning stages of formation. It is not that offenses disappear, but their lifespan inside the mind shortens. They are seen sooner, recognized earlier, and released before they become fully formed emotional cycles. This is where forgiveness stops behaving like an intervention and starts becoming a pattern of life.

Releasing Before the Mind Fully Engages

One of the most noticeable changes in this stage is the reduction of delay between feeling and awareness. In earlier phases, emotional reactions could develop quietly in the background before becoming fully conscious. Now, there is a kind of internal sensitivity that recognizes early signals of disturbance. This recognition interrupts the natural expansion of emotional reactivity.

Instead of building a full narrative around an offense, the mind begins to step back almost immediately after noticing it. There is a moment of recognition where engagement could continue, but does not. That moment becomes increasingly familiar. Over time, it becomes less of a struggle and more of an instinctive redirection.

This does not mean emotions stop appearing. They still surface, but they no longer automatically grow into extended internal conversations. What changes is the relationship to them. They are observed earlier in their formation, which prevents them from becoming structurally dominant inside the mind. Forgiveness, in this sense, becomes less about repair and more about interruption of escalation.

The result is a quieter inner environment where emotional reactions no longer dictate the full structure of thought. Life continues, but the internal processing of life becomes less reactive and more contained.

Gratitude as a Reorientation of Attention

At this stage, gratitude does not appear as a forced practice or emotional exercise. It emerges more naturally as attention begins to shift away from internal accumulation of unresolved emotional material. When the mind is no longer occupied with constant replay of past injury, it becomes more capable of noticing what is present without distortion.

This shift is subtle at first. It is not that difficult circumstances disappear or that challenges become less real. Instead, attention stops being monopolized by what is unresolved. The mind begins to register ordinary moments again without immediately filtering them through past emotional experience. This creates a different kind of perception, one that is less narrowed by internal conflict.

Gratitude begins to appear in small recognitions rather than large emotional declarations. It is found in the absence of constant internal pressure, in the reduction of emotional noise, and in the ability to experience a moment without it being overshadowed by memory. Over time, this becomes less of a practice and more of a default orientation.

The internal world becomes less defined by what is missing or what was wrong, and more capable of holding what simply is. This does not erase difficulty, but it changes the center of attention away from it.

Self-Reflection Without Self-Punishment

Another transformation begins to appear in how the mind relates to itself. Earlier stages often involved intense internal examination, where thoughts about past actions, responses, or reactions could easily turn into cycles of judgment or regret. In this stage, reflection remains, but its tone changes.

The mind begins to observe itself without immediately turning observation into condemnation. This is not avoidance of responsibility, but a shift in how awareness functions internally. There is more space between noticing something and emotionally reacting to it. That space allows clarity to enter before judgment takes over.

Self-reflection becomes more about understanding patterns than punishing behavior. Instead of asking why something went wrong in a way that leads to emotional collapse, the mind begins to ask what pattern is forming and how it can be interrupted earlier next time. The focus shifts from emotional weight to structural awareness.

This change creates a more stable internal environment. Reflection no longer destabilizes the self; it organizes it. Awareness becomes a tool for adjustment rather than a source of internal conflict.

When Forgiveness Becomes the Default Response

Eventually, something more integrated begins to emerge. Forgiveness is no longer something applied after emotional disturbance, but something that quietly influences the initial response to disturbance itself. The gap between trigger and reaction becomes wide enough for awareness to intervene naturally.

This does not mean the absence of difficulty or emotional challenge. It means the internal system has learned a different rhythm. Instead of reacting first and processing later, there is a growing tendency to pause internally before reaction fully develops. In that pause, old patterns lose their automatic control.

What replaces them is not perfection, but flexibility. The mind is no longer locked into a single way of responding to emotional disruption. There is room for adjustment, reconsideration, and release before escalation becomes structure.

Forgiveness, at this stage, is not dramatic. It is quiet, repetitive, and woven into ordinary experience. It appears in how quickly the mind recovers, how lightly it holds emotional impressions, and how naturally it returns to balance after disturbance.

A Life That No Longer Carries Its Own Weight

As this way of living becomes more consistent, something subtle but profound takes place. Life is still complex, still unpredictable, still full of human interaction and emotional variability. But the internal burden carried through those experiences is no longer the same.

The mind does not accumulate emotional weight in the same way it once did. Experiences pass through awareness without remaining as prolonged internal residue. The system learns not to store every emotional impression at full intensity.

This creates a kind of internal lightness that is difficult to describe in abstract terms, but clear in experience. Life continues, but it no longer feels like it is being carried entirely within the emotional system. There is space within the mind that remains unaffected even while experiences come and go.

Forgiveness, in this final sense, is not an action repeated only in moments of conflict. It becomes a way of existing in which emotional release is faster than emotional accumulation. The inner world no longer builds permanent structures out of temporary experiences.

And in that quiet restructuring, life becomes lighter—not because it is easier, but because it is no longer carried in the same way.

Chapter 17: The Invitation to Freedom

On June 17, 2015, the tragedy at Mother Emanuel AME Church in Charleston, South Carolina had already entered the national memory of the United States. In the courtroom days later, on June 19, 2015, families of the victims stood face to face with the man responsible, **Dylann Roof**, during his bond hearing. Among them was Nadine Collier, daughter of Ethel Lance, one of the nine people killed in the attack.

Her statement that day became one of the most widely reported moments of the proceedings. She spoke about her mother, her loss, and the emptiness that followed. Then she said something that surprised many who were watching: she chose to forgive. Not because the pain was gone, not because the event made sense, but because she no longer wanted to carry the weight of hatred inside her life.

What often gets missed in how this moment is remembered is what it reveals about human choice at the deepest level. There was no external pressure forcing forgiveness. There was no immediate emotional relief that made it easy. In fact, everything in the situation naturally leaned toward the opposite direction: grief, anger, and irreversible loss. Yet in that space, a personal decision was made about what would be carried forward internally.

In the years that followed, families connected to the Charleston tragedy continued to speak publicly in memorials, interviews, and community gatherings. What became clear over time was that forgiveness, for many of them, was not a single emotional conclusion but an ongoing question they had to live with: What kind of life will I build from here, and what will I refuse to let define me anymore?

Psychological research on long-term grief and trauma response shows that after catastrophic loss, the human mind often returns repeatedly to the same emotional material. Even when initial decisions are made to release anger or resentment, the memory does not stop appearing. What changes is the response to it. Over time, individuals who find stability are often those who learn to separate memory from identity, and pain from direction.

In Nadine Collier's public words and later reflections from other Charleston families, there is a consistent pattern that appears in trauma recovery studies as well: freedom does not arrive as a single emotional moment, but as a repeated invitation to stop re-entering internal cycles of suffering. Each time memory returns, a new internal choice is quietly presented—continue carrying it in the same way, or release its hold again.

This is where the idea of invitation becomes important. Freedom is not forced onto a person, and it is not completed by one decision alone. It is offered repeatedly in the ordinary moments of life when memory returns without warning. A photograph, a date, a conversation, a quiet thought—each becomes a point where the inner world can either reopen old wounds or step away from them again.

In Charleston, this reality became visible not in the courtroom alone, but in the years that followed. Families continued living, speaking, rebuilding, and remembering. The past did not disappear, but it also did not remain the only place they lived internally. Something shifted from being trapped inside the event to standing outside of it while still remembering it.

Chapter 17 begins here: at the moment when forgiveness is no longer only about the past, but about the present choice to no longer be defined by what the past demands. It is the quiet invitation that returns again and again, asking one simple question in different forms: are you willing to be free, even now?

When the Teaching Turns Into a Question

By the time a reader reaches this point, the material is no longer trying to explain forgiveness as an abstract idea. Something quieter is happening now. The focus shifts away from description and begins to lean directly into personal recognition. It is no longer about understanding forgiveness in general terms, but about noticing where life itself is still being shaped by what has not been released.

There is a subtle discomfort that can arise in this stage, because clarity tends to remove the distance that earlier reflection provided. What once felt like theory now begins to feel closer to lived reality. The mind cannot stay fully in observation anymore; it begins to turn inward and ask whether anything in this journey actually belongs to the reader's own life experience. That shift is where reflection becomes personal responsibility.

At this point, silence itself becomes meaningful. Not the absence of thought, but the presence of recognition that does not immediately translate into escape. The material no longer stands in front of the reader; it begins to stand *with* the reader, asking to be answered in lived experience rather than analysis.

When the Question Becomes Personal

There is a moment where the text cannot continue without turning into reflection that belongs to the reader alone. The question is no longer general. It becomes specific in an internal way that does not require external detail to be understood. Somewhere in memory, in relationship, or in unresolved emotional space, there are figures that naturally surface when forgiveness is mentioned.

At this stage, the mind begins to do something it may not have done earlier with the same honesty: it begins to connect teaching with actual life weight. Not in theory, but in emotional consequence. The question does not accuse; it reveals. Who remains internally active in thought even when they are no longer present in daily life. Who still occupies space in emotional response even when time has passed.

And alongside that question comes another that is more uncomfortable, because it shifts attention away from the other person and toward internal experience itself. What is being carried by continuing to hold this? Not in moral language, but in lived cost. What does it take from attention, from peace, from mental availability, from the ability to move through life without background tension.

At this level, awareness becomes less about interpretation and more about recognition. The reader is no longer being guided toward a concept, but toward a mirror that does not soften what it reflects.

When Cost Becomes Visible Without Explanation

There is a kind of clarity that does not arrive through reasoning but through accumulated experience. The cost of unresolved emotional holding is rarely immediate; it is gradual, subtle, and often normalized over time. It shows itself in patterns rather than events, in internal tension rather than external disruption.

When attention is no longer constantly occupied with replaying or defending emotional memory, something else becomes noticeable: how much energy was previously tied to it. Not in dramatic exhaustion, but in background consumption of mental space. The mind begins to recognize that certain thoughts were not neutral—they were sustained effort.

This recognition does not require exaggeration of pain or reinforcement of suffering. It simply becomes visible that internal freedom is not only about letting go of a past moment, but about releasing the ongoing internal maintenance that the memory required. That maintenance has a cost, even when it is not consciously acknowledged.

And so the question becomes less abstract and more grounded in lived awareness. Not whether forgiveness is correct or justified, but whether continued holding is still quietly shaping the present in ways that are no longer desired.

When Freedom Is No Longer a Concept but a Direction

By the end of this reflection, something shifts that does not depend on emotional intensity or dramatic decision. The idea of freedom stops appearing as something distant or ideal and begins to feel like a direction the inner life can move toward without contradiction.

There is no pressure in this movement, no force pushing toward emotional performance. Instead, there is a simple recognition that carrying certain internal weights is no longer required for identity, meaning, or protection. The space that opens from that recognition does not demand immediate action, but it does remove confusion about possibility.

Freedom begins to take shape not as escape from memory, but as release from its control over present experience. Life does not need to be rewritten for this shift to matter. It simply begins to feel different from the inside, less constrained by what no longer needs to define it.

And so the invitation is not presented as demand, but as awareness that has become difficult to ignore. Not everyone from the past needs to remain active in the present. Not every memory needs to continue shaping emotional reality. And not every weight that has been carried is still necessary to carry.

What remains is not instruction, but recognition: that freedom has already begun wherever holding is no longer required to feel whole.

www.ingramcontent.com/pod-product-compliance
Ingram Content Group UK Ltd.
Pitfield, Milton Keynes, MK11 3LW, UK
UKHW021401190726
13845UKWH00028B/817

9 788168 642935